T0361230

A Practical Guide to

Planning for E-Business Success

How to E-Enable Your Enterprise

A Practical Guide to

Planning for
E-Business Success

How to E-Enable Your Enterprise

Anita Cassidy

Taylor & Francis
Taylor & Francis Group

Boca Raton   London   New York   Singapore

A CRC title, part of the Taylor & Francis imprint, a member of the
Taylor & Francis Group, the academic division of T&F Informa plc.

Library of Congress Cataloging-in-Publication Data

Cassidy, Anita.
    A practical guide to planning for E-business success : how to E-enable your enterprise /
by Anita Cassidy.
        p. cm.
    Includes index.
    ISBN 1-57444-304-6 (alk. paper)
    1. Electronic commerce. 2. Business enterprises—Computer network resources. 3.
Business planning. 4. Internet. I. Title: Guide to planning for E-business success. II.
Title: Planning for E-business success. III. Title.
HF5548.32 .C377 2001
658'.054678—dc21   2001041872

Visit the CRC Press Web site at www.crcpress.com

© 2002 by CRC Press

No claim to original U.S. Government works
International Standard Book Number 1-57444-304-6
Library of Congress Card Number 2001041872

PREFACE

The Internet has had, and will continue to have, a major impact on our lives and businesses. It changes everything. The Internet provides a means to transform entire industries, create new industries, challenge industry leaders, and enable business in entirely new ways. Companies use the Internet to expand their markets, increase revenue, streamline processes, and increase the speed of business. The Internet is a valuable tool to help meet customer expectations. It is no longer a matter of **if** companies will participate in the Internet revolution, but rather **when** and **how**.

The majority of companies today have some sort of Internet presence. This presence may only be basic marketing information about the company, or it may allow customers to transmit simple orders over the Internet. However, after the initial rush to establish an Internet presence, many companies are now asking how they can shift to true e-business and use this powerful technology to actually provide them with a competitive advantage in the marketplace.

The new era requires organizations to think and act differently than they have in the past. Companies are able to gain a competitive edge by integrating their e-business strategies into their overall business strategies and letting customer needs drive their business strategies. Although technology is a key enabler, the business strategy is the core foundation. Companies must carefully plan use of this critical technology.

E-business is a business endeavor, not a technical endeavor. Companies have become e-enabled by tightly integrating the Internet throughout their core business processes. They integrate people, processes, and technology to transform the entire business model. Successful companies know their customers, know their business, and plan. They are flexible and agile, prepared to anticipate and react quickly to changes.

Rather than just talking about the Internet hype, this book provides a step-by-step guide to developing a solid e-business strategy that is based on the overall business strategy. The book is organized into 11 chapters that lead you through the development of a complete e-business plan. Examples, checklists, questions, and templates are provided to help begin and guide your efforts.

Chapter 1 provides an introduction to e-business. It begins by reviewing the impact of technology on businesses today. The chapter provides an overview of e-business within the context of business, application, and technology trends. The chapter discusses some of the hurdles or barriers to successful e-business implementations as well as some of the key lessons learned by companies that have entered e-business. The chapter emphasizes the importance of and need for planning to ensure your e-business ventures are successful.

Chapter 2 provides an overview of the eight phases in developing an e-business strategy. It discusses the key principles that are the foundation for the methodology.

Chapters 3 through 10 detail the steps of the e-business planning methodology. Chapter 3 outlines how to **begin** the e-business planning process by obtaining executive support, defining the purpose, identifying the team, defining the planning process and communication plan, and announcing the effort. Chapter 4 offers guidance to **diagnose** trends, the current environment, stakeholders, the stakeholder processes, industry impact, value chain, and business impact. Chapter 5 provides a process to **develop** the value proposition, value delivery proposition, strategy, and key metrics for measuring success. Chapter 6 outlines how to **define** opportunities, the competitive situation, and priorities. Chapter 7 details steps to **determine** the impact e-business will have on the application architecture, technical architecture, information systems processes, business processes, people, and organization. A cost/benefit analysis and a detailed implementation roadmap are prepared. Chapter 8 suggests guidelines for the **design** of the e-business solution, including the look and feel, navigation, screen design, application design, and security. Chapter 9 outlines suggestions as you **deliver** the e-business solution. Chapter 10 explains how to **discuss** the results of the e-business implementation by obtaining feedback, analyzing, and determining the appropriate action.

Chapter 11 summarizes the methodology. Appendix A contains a reference list of questions to ask during each phase of the methodology. Although it is not necessary to document answers to each question in the e-business planning effort, the questions are meant to provoke discussion and thought in your organization. Tailor the questions to your specific needs and situation.

This book is intended for business and information systems managers interested in moving their companies into the new e-business era. Chief Information Officers (CIO) or Information Systems executives will find this book especially helpful in guiding their e-business initiatives. E-business initiatives are often led by executives within the business as successful e-business implementations cross all business functions. As such, an in-depth or detailed technical background is not necessary to benefit from this book. This book and the methodology presented can be utilized for a traditional brick-and-mortar company venturing into e-business as well as born-on-the-Web dot com companies.

I sincerely hope this book helps ensure the success of your e-business journey.

ACKNOWLEDGMENTS

As with my first two books, I wish to thank many people for their encouragement, advice, insight, and support while I was writing this book:

- My husband, Dan, who is the definition of a truly supportive spouse. He assisted in the development of the concepts and endless reviews of this book.
- My sons, Mike and Ryan, for their patience and support while the book was being written. I look forward to watching and learning from them as they grow in this new e-business world.
- My friend, Stephanie Renslow, for her endless support and friendship.
- My mom, who provides continuous support and help, and in memory of my dad, who taught me the value of working hard and continuously learning.
- Keith Guggenberger, who helped formulate many of the ideas presented in this book, edited, and assisted in the writing of the book.
- Several colleagues who have provided input and reviewed the book, including Steven Haas, Scott Peterson, Dan Christian, Dick Thon, Cheryl Nordby, and Betty Juntune.
- The numerous people I have worked with who have helped develop the ideas presented in this book.
- You, the reader, as it is YOU who have the power to take advantage of this new e-business era and obtain a competitive advantage in the marketplace.

Anita Cassidy

THE AUTHOR

Anita Cassidy has more than 25 years of experience in Information Systems. She is President/CEO of Strategic Computing Directions Incorporated in Minneapolis, Minnesota, an executive information systems consulting company specializing in strategic planning, e-business strategy, information systems assessment, temporary leadership, and process reengineering (www.strategiccomputing.com). She has been Vice President and Chief Information Officer of a worldwide manufacturing company, Director of Information Systems of a medical device manufacturing company, and Director of several divisions of a Fortune 100 instrument engineering and manufacturing company. Ms. Cassidy has a Bachelor of Science degree from the University of Minnesota and also attended St. Cloud State University. She has written two books, *A Practical Guide to Information Systems Strategic Planning* (1998) and, with Keith Guggenberger, *A Practical Guide to Information Systems Process Improvement* (2000), both published by St. Lucie Press.

CONTENTS

1

INTRODUCTION
TO E-BUSINESS

"Slumber not in the tents of your fathers. The world is advancing. Advance with it."

Giuseppe Mazzini

TECHNOLOGY REVOLUTION

The Internet has dramatically changed the role of technology in businesses today. A survey conducted by A.T. Kearney of 251 global CEOs identified technology as the number one CEO concern.* Not long ago, technology and information systems were seen by many as a necessary evil of the organization to report financial results but only providing minimal return on investment. Times have definitely changed! As the A.T. Kearney 2000 CEO survey shows, technology has become a fundamental driver of the business strategy and 97% of the CEOs surveyed felt that technology will have an extremely or moderately important role in the future success of their companies. In fact, 78% of the North American executives surveyed stated that the Internet has already changed how they do business. Technology is no longer just an enabler; it has become a vital part of business.

The Internet has been adopted faster than any previous technology. As shown in Figure 1.1, it took 38 years for the radio to reach 50 million users, 16 years for the PC, 13 years for television, and only 4 years for

---

* A.T. Kearney (an EDS company), "Strategic Information Technology and the CEO Agenda," www.atkearney.com, 2000.

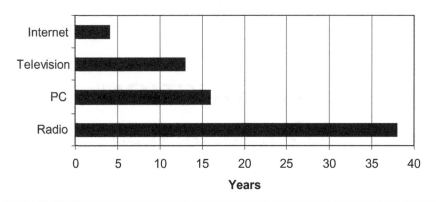

Figure 1.1   Years for Technologies to Reach 50 Million Users

the Internet.* The Internet has transformed the information industry in much the same ways as the automobile and airplane transformed travel. The key to future success is not merely using the Internet, but re-inventing business models and business processes using this new technology.

In early 1998, forecasters suggested that business-to-business e-business might rise to $300B by 2002. Most forecasters now consider that estimate to be too low. As Figure 1.2,** shows Forester Research estimates that business-to-business e-business will rise to $1.823 trillion by 2003. Gartner Group predicts that business-to-business transactions will reach $7.3 trillion by 2004.*** According to Uunet (an Internet backbone provider), traffic on the Internet continues to double every 100 days. Approximately 235,000 sites are added each month, or one new domain every 9 minutes. Most historians and forecasters consider this incredible explosion the largest revolution in history, even more significant than the Industrial Revolution. Economic models are shifting overnight and industry leaders are challenged in new and unpredictable ways every day. The Internet and e-business are described as a disruptive technology, rather than an adaptive technology, because they change the way that businesses operate and interact with business partners. Economic models are shifting overnight. Industry leaders are challenged in new and unpredictable ways every day. Entire industries are being reshaped.

---

* Norris, Grant, Hurley, James R., Hartley, Kenneth M., Dunleavy, John R., and Balls, John D., *E-Business and ERP,* Wiley, 2000, p. 10. Also stated by U.S. Department of Commerce, Spring 1998.

** Forrester Research, in "E-commerce revenues set to explode," *InfoWorld,* May 8, 2000.

***Kao, Chuck, "Enterprise Application Portals," *eAI Journal,* February 2001, p. 49.

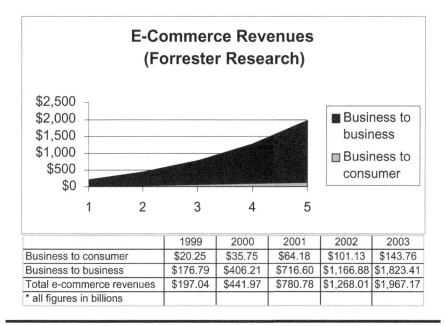

	1999	2000	2001	2002	2003
Business to consumer	$20.25	$35.75	$64.18	$101.13	$143.76
Business to business	$176.79	$406.21	$716.60	$1,166.88	$1,823.41
Total e-commerce revenues	$197.04	$441.97	$780.78	$1,268.01	$1,967.17
* all figures in billions					

Figure 1.2   E-Commerce Projected Revenues (Forrester Research)

E-BUSINESS OVERVIEW

As the Internet has rapidly become a critical component of our lives, it is important to take a step back and understand the meaning of e-business and the various overused labels. Some people confuse the Internet, e-commerce, and e-business to mean the same thing. The Internet is the tool or vehicle. E-commerce is merely transacting (buying or selling) over the Internet or other electronic means. E-business uses Internet technologies to improve all business processes and activities within a business as well as processes that reach out to the stakeholders of the company. E-business is the integration of people, processes, and technology to conduct business. It uses technology to build global business processes, relationships, and commerce. Some may refer to this as e-enabling the enterprise or e-enterprise. To simplify matters, I will refer to the entire Internet integration of an enterprise as e-business. A company's e-business environment may include an Internet that is accessible to the general public, an Extranet that is accessible only to certain individuals with proper security, or an Intranet that is accessible to employees and internal individuals.

E-business is not just putting out a Web page. E-business encompasses the entire business model of a company (business to employees, customers, suppliers, partners, and value chain), as shown in Figure 1.3.

E-Business Encompasses the Entire Business Model

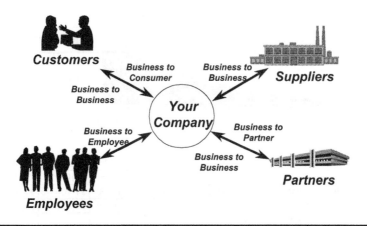

Figure 1.3   E-Business Encompasses the Entire Business Model

E-business impacts the relationships between customers, manufacturers, and suppliers. Common acronyms include:

- **B2B:** Business-to-business, or automating the transactions between businesses. For example, inventory is checked automatically or even by the supplier to ensure enough parts are on hand to meet forecasted needs. If there are not enough parts, an automated order for the necessary parts is sent to the approved suppliers. The parts are shipped in time to meet the demand. Later, invoices and payments are transacted electronically. The business result is an event-driven environment driven by demand. B2B processing has many benefits. Reductions in inventory, manufacturing cycle time, and overhead costs can be realized. Defects and quality issues can be reacted to quickly, before building costly inventory. B2B allows a business to expand its reach globally. Customer and partner loyalty can also be increased through ease of use, greater efficiency of transactions, and personalization.
- **B2C:** Business-to-consumer, or automating the consumer purchasing process. For example, the process may begin with an online campaign to interest the consumer. Customers visit the Web site, research the products, place their orders online, provide online payment via credit card, and receive electronic order confirmation. Customers can check

the status of their orders online as well as address any order issues or questions. Customers receive their orders, can handle returns online, register the products, receive maintenance notifications, and obtain support through an online support center. There are many benefits to a B2C process such as increased customer satisfaction, increased speed of transaction from order to ship, decreased cost of sales, and decreased customer support costs. In the consumer banking industry, the costs of completing a transaction have gone from $1.05/transaction just a few years ago to under $0.02/transaction using the Internet.* Popular B2C models include e-tailing (www.amazon.com), consumer portals (www.autoconnect.com), bidding and auctioning (www.ebay.com, www.onsale.com), consumer care, customer management, invoicing, and electronic bill payment.

■ **B2E:** Business-to-employee, or providing necessary information to internal employees via an Intranet. Examples include company information, self-management of benefits, and internal process and procedure documentation and forms. B2E is a critical component for B2B to work properly. If this is not in place, B2B does not reap the full benefits.

■ **A2A:** Anyone-to-anyone, allows any entity to be able to do business with any other entity. A2A includes business-to-business and business-to-consumer, as well as consumer-to-consumer, business-to-exchange, and many other relationships. Chat boards or consumer bidding sites are examples of anyone-to-anyone interactions.

E-business enables businesses to re-invent themselves and do business in entirely new ways. E-business changes the competitive landscape and distribution channels. It expands the marketplace, extends market reach, and increases revenue. E-business streamlines interactions, increases the speed of business, and increases the expectations of customers. As Figure 1.4 shows, e-business can impact market share, make successful companies, and kill companies that are slow to adjust.

Successful companies of the future will be entirely e-enabled so that the Internet initiatives are inseparable from the rest of the company and tightly integrated in all their core business processes. These companies will not assume that the business model that made them successful in the past will carry them into the future. To successfully make the transition from e-business to a truly e-enabled enterprise, a company must begin by understanding its customers and anticipating trends in business, business applications, and technology.

---

* Klasson, Kirk, "Business Models for the New Economy," Cambridge Technology Partners White Paper, Cambridge, MA, 2000, p. 12, www.ctp.com/wwt.

E-Business...

Is NOT...	It uses technology to...
Just putting out a Web page or just Web-enabling existing applications	• **Redefine business, maximize customer value, enable business in new ways** • **Change the competitive landscape, distribution channels** • **Impact market share, extend market reach** • **Increase the speed of business, streamline interactions, increase expectations of the customers** • **Make and kill companies**

Figure 1.4   E-Business Is Not...

E-Business Sets New Requirements

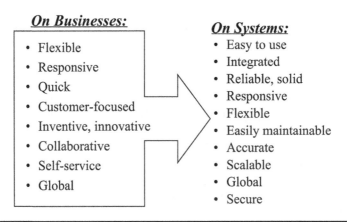

On Businesses:
- Flexible
- Responsive
- Quick
- Customer-focused
- Inventive, innovative
- Collaborative
- Self-service
- Global

On Systems:
- Easy to use
- Integrated
- Reliable, solid
- Responsive
- Flexible
- Easily maintainable
- Accurate
- Scalable
- Global
- Secure

Figure 1.5   E-Business Requirements

BUSINESS TRENDS

The Internet revolution is having a major impact on businesses and information systems today. The changes require businesses to operate very differently than in the past. As Figure 1.5 shows, these changes place new requirements and expectations on information systems. Businesses must be

A Paradigm Shift

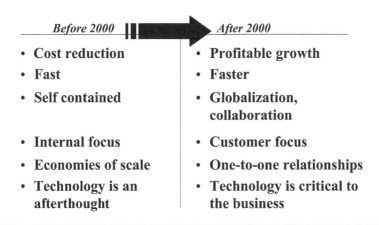

Before 2000	*After 2000*
• Cost reduction	• **Profitable growth**
• Fast	• **Faster**
• Self contained	• **Globalization, collaboration**
• Internal focus	• **Customer focus**
• Economies of scale	• **One-to-one relationships**
• Technology is an afterthought	• **Technology is critical to the business**

Figure 1.6   Paradigm Shift in Business Trends

flexible, quick, customer-focused, innovative, collaborative, and global, and allow self-service. In fact, the A.T. Kearney CEO survey identified customer orientation, flexibility, and using technology well to be the top three critical success factors for the future.* Technology and systems must be easy to use, integrated, reliable, responsive, flexible, easy to maintain, accurate, scaleable, global, and secure.

In a sense, e-business is a cultural revolution. Critical business trends impacted by this paradigm shift, as shown in Figure 1.6, include:

■ **Shift from a cost reduction strategy to a business growth strategy:** In the past, most companies focused on cost reduction. Many of their projects focused on improving business efficiencies. The previous technology focus of implementing new Enterprise Requirements Planning (ERP) systems was largely seen as a way for companies to reduce costs and improve efficiencies. These efforts were effective because they typically used technology to replace manual efforts with computer processes that reduced manpower, thus lowering overhead costs. With the changing competitive landscape and changing distribution channels, companies are using the Internet to capture market share, expand geographical coverage, and increase sales growth. Projects are shifting from cost-reduction

---

* A.T. Kearney (an EDS company), "Strategic Information Technology and the CEO Agenda," www.atkearney.com, 2000.

efforts to investments for growth. Many dot com companies rose to popularity and quickly failed in the 1999–2000 time frame because they focused solely on growth rather than costs. If traditional management fundamentals prove true, to be successful over the long term, the focus must be on a balanced approach of cost reduction as well as revenue growth.

■ **Increased speed of doing business:** Companies are moving from fast to faster. There is an increased speed of doing everything. With technology changes and the Internet, customer expectations are changing. Customers want everything faster. Increased customer demands place new demands on businesses to be faster. Customer expectations are reshaping operational requirements for businesses. Business agility is a key to success in the new era. In the past, change and speed caused turmoil and chaos. Now, change and speed spell opportunity! The speed of processes in companies is changing from calendar time to Internet time. Companies are shifting from a focus on long-range planning to shorter planning cycles with quick execution. Rather than predicting the future, companies are learning to react to the future using technology.

■ **Shift from self-containment to globalization:** With the Internet, companies are becoming global overnight. Small companies have the same opportunities as large companies to capture global markets. In the past, functional departments, plants, sales territories, or countries would operate as individual independent self-contained silos. They could operate with different information, definitions, languages, cultures, and objectives. Now, there are no boundaries and separate entities must function as a single global organization to be effective.

■ **Increased collaboration:** The Internet is causing companies to be more collaborative among themselves, and even with competitors, to deliver a complete solution to the customer. Rather than linear and sequential supply chains, the markets are changing to networked webs of value. This new market is shown in Figure 1.7. In the new market, it is critical to have integrated information across an enterprise (even throughout the supply chain). No longer can companies have separate systems, platforms, and information silos. Rather than self-contained information, there is supply chain information sharing. It is critical that a company identify what it does best, or the core business value proposition, and select partners to outsource what it does not do best. A virtual organization of collaborative partners is created that can change if needed. There is an increase in the number of alliances and partnerships that a company needs to be successful in the marketplace. Supply chains are changing from being strictly linear to webs of common interest.

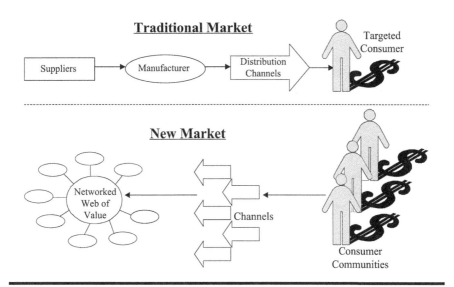

Figure 1.7 Traditional vs. New Market

Companies are combining goods and services into new bundles for a one-stop source. Some examples of various collaboration or exchanges include:

— www.autoconnect.com tries to handle everything car-related
— www.quicken.com tries to handle all financial needs for banking, mortgage, retirement, investment, and insurance
— www.altranet.com facilitates trade for the utilities industry
— www.ratexchange.com facilitates public carriers and private companies to trade telecommunications capacity
— www.commerxplasticsnet.com facilitates trade for the plastics industry
— www.necx.com is a online exchange site for electronics
— www.rosettanet.org is for electronic components and IT industries
— www.vics.org is for the retail industry
— www.fmi.org is for the grocery industry
— www.ehcr.org is for the healthcare products industry
— www.efr-central.com is for the food service industry
— www.seafood.com is for buying and selling of seafood

As this list shows, there are many different types of exchanges, including storefronts, infomediaries, brokers, communities of interest or commerce, portals, and intermediaries. A strength of the online grocers (such as www.simondelivers.com) is that they can provide products from multiple companies; Bruggers Bagels and

HoneyBaked Ham can be delivered at the same time with milk and cereal from the grocery store, all in one stop. Companies are even collaborating with their customers. Microsoft distributed the beta version of Windows 2000 to more than 650,000 software engineers who tested the product and provided feedback.

■ **Move from economies of scale to one-to-one relationships:** In the past, to reduce costs companies would produce large quantities of the same item. In the new era, custom-tailoring products to the individual needs of each customer is important. Make-to-order rather than mass make-to-stock is increasing in importance. Tailoring communications to the individual needs of each customer is critical. Mass marketing is changing to mass customization. Companies such as Amazon (www.amazon.com) and Drugstore.com (www.drugstore.com) collect and analyze customer buying patterns so that they can tailor the marketing of products to the needs and desires of individual customers. For example, if Amazon sees a customer likes books on e-business, it notifies the customer when new e-business books are published. If a customer typically purchases Vitamin C from www.drugstore.com, the company notifies the customer when it has a sale on the product. Ritz Carlton hotels implemented a global computerized service based on specific customer profiles of key customers. Guests can specify preferences such as a room away from the elevator, foam pillow, a glass of White Zinfandel at night, and the *Wall Street Journal* in the morning. Although companies may have front-end business applications with customized one-to-one delivery, many have common back-end systems for efficiencies provided through outsourcing or centralization. The Internet makes location less important and connectivity both cost effective and reliable. For example, many different companies may outsource to the same call center provider. The script is customized by company, and personalized e-mails may be sent. The operations process is more standardized while the service to the customer is more customized.

■ **Shift from internal focus to external focus:** Companies are looking outside the walls of the corporation and reaching out to the customers. Companies today are giving the customers what they want rather than telling them what they can have, as in the past. With the assistance of tools such as Customer Relationship Management (CRM), companies are becoming customer-focused. Rather than building to inventory, some companies are shifting to build to a specific customer order. For example, Dell (www.dell.com) is focusing its strategy less on the actual hardware and placing more emphasis on the ability to configure to exact needs and deliver the hardware to the customer's door. In addition to wanting products faster, customers want everything better and cheaper. Customers are more knowledgeable and empowered. More than 70% of automobile sales in 1999 were made to consumers who researched their purchases on the Internet.* A survey by Deloitte Research of 900 executives in 35 countries concluded that manufacturers would be 60% more profitable if they became customer-centered.**

■ **Shift to customer self-service:** Consumers are more educated and computer literate than ever before. Rather than an attitude of "let the customer beware," the customer is becoming the most powerful force. Customers are willing to help themselves and obtain information directly, and companies are providing facilities to encourage self-service. Providing self-service can make better use of everyone's time such as checking and ordering flights and hotels on-line rather than through a travel agent or making price comparisons. A good example of a company providing self-service through the Internet is Whirlpool (www.whirlpool.com). The consumers can assist themselves by trouble-shooting and diagnosing issues with appliances and receive recommended solutions or replacement parts. The customers can complete the repairs themselves. Cisco Systems provides an online service database that enables customers to solve problems encountered by other customers.

■ **Increased importance of processes:** As the need to react faster while maintaining quality continues to be critical, companies are realizing the importance of having integrated, efficient, and effective processes. A company's customer satisfaction is only as good as its internal processes. Rather than having large structured processes, flexibility and adaptability are key to designing processes. In July 2000, the Federal Trade Commission fined seven Internet companies a total of $1.5M because they did not have proper business processes in place to handle orders and notify customers of problems during the 1999 Christmas season.*** Under federal law (the Mail and Telephone Order Rule), Internet merchants must deliver items by the time they specify or within 30 days of the order if no delivery time is stated. If they cannot deliver, they must have processes in place to notify customers and give them a chance to

---

* Prahalad, C.K., Ramaswamy, Venkatram, and Krishnan, M.S., "Consumer Centricity," *Information Week*, April 10, 2000, p. 74, www.informationweek.com.
** "Making Customer Loyalty Real: Lessons from Leading Manufacturers," *CIO Magazine*, Section 1, October 1, 1999, Deloitte Research (www.dc.com/research).
***Bacheldor, Beth and Konicki, Steve, "Long Arm of the Law," *Information Week*, August 7, 2000, p. 24.

cancel their orders. With e-business, businesses are finding they are exposing their key processes beyond the boundaries of the corporation's four walls to global customers, suppliers, stakeholders, partners, and competitors.

■ **Shift to virtual office:** Although labor markets have been volatile since the NASDAQ crash, forecasts for experienced resources are tight. Companies are doing what they can to keep employees satisfied. Virtual offices are increasing as technology enables business any time and anywhere. This shift demands that companies have not only the technology, but also well-defined business processes in place. Someone who works out of the home needs to have the appearance of being at work to customers. Virtual offices have the power to support most business functions today, except for the manufacture of products. Eliminating large offices reduces overhead and provides a savings to the customer. It reduces travel on busy highways, reduces the number of parking spaces required, reduces the fuel and energy required for transportation and heating of offices, and enables a higher quality of life for employees. The future is using limited resources wisely, providing the best service possible to customers, and operating with the highest return to stakeholders.

■ **Changing organizational structures:** To remain competitive, companies are merging, acquiring, and divesting more than ever in the past. Organizations and organizational structures are changing overnight. Dot com companies are emerging and dissolving, and companies are spinning off Internet-based initiatives. The pendulum will continue to swing and organizations must be flexible. Companies are changing their organization structures to focus on groups of customers rather than on products.

■ **Information systems and technology is a critical enabler to business rather than an afterthought:** Information systems are an increasingly important component to the production and value delivery process. Companies are using technology to reinvent the business and maximize customer value. E-business is a critical enabler of business to provide a competitive edge in the market. Rather than just processing data and transactions, companies are truly using information to create knowledge. Rather than just using technology to create and document products as they flow through the process, technology is controlling the flow of information and products. Rather than just finding value in tangible assets such as building and products, value is found in relationships, branding, integration, and information. For example, FedEx (www.fedex.com) has a global network for moving shipments. However, its business strategy and actions emphasize that information about each shipment is as valuable as the shipment itself. Wal-Mart (www.walmart.com) is another example of a company that has placed as much value on sharing and moving information to secure a competitive advantage as it has on the products themselves. With technology improvements (cheaper, more powerful, higher bandwidth, higher reliability), technology is everywhere in an enterprise.

In addition to enabling new business, the Internet and technology are enabling a reinvention of the business mindset. Today's commerce has evolved from the industrial revolution of the early 1900s when mass transportation, mass communication, and mass production were the name of the game. As the population grew, bigger was better. Tomorrow's success takes a different road. Intangibles are becoming more important. Although the creation and consumption of goods are key to today's economic growth, in the future, consumption will need to be tempered with the limitation of natural resources and a continued thirst for a balanced lifestyle. The computer and the Internet are the foundations for reinventing how we do business and how we communicate. E-business is expanding and breaking down walls for enlightened communication.

It is important for companies to recognize how these general business trends impact their e-business strategies and plans, but the trends will also impact how their customers in a business-to-business environment may be changing. These changes may impact the business success of a company that has a strategy based on old paradigms. Cambridge Technology Partners (www.ctp.com) identified how the business model is morphing:*

> *We are going from a period marked by large hierarchies that were self-contained value-producing and value-exchanging entities whose economies of scope lowered transaction and coordination costs*

> *...to a period marked by narrowly focused value-creating entities networked together based on well understood boundaries of complementary skills sets*

> *...to a community of hyper-competitive value-creating entities networked together by specialized value-exchanging entities, or e-markets, serving highly informed and empowered customers.*

It is indeed an exciting time!

---

* Klasson, Kirk, "Business Models for the New Economy," Cambridge Technology Partners White Paper, Cambridge, MA, 2000, p. 6, www.ctp.com/wwt.

BUSINESS APPLICATION TRENDS

As Figure 1.8 shows, many business applications are enabled or enhanced by Internet technologies. These trends include:

- **Enterprise Requirements Planning (ERP):** Although ERP is not getting the press and hype that it received in the late 1990s, ERP continues to be of utmost importance and has become a basic assumption to doing business. For a truly e-enabled enterprise, quality information must be available anywhere it is needed in real time. Information scattered in various islands of information hinders the development of e-business as it:
  — Increases costs
  — Decreases accuracy
  — Increases processing and development time
  — Reduces flexibility

  As companies are Internet enabling (or e-enabling) applications, it is becoming painfully clear how important it is to have an integrated and fully functioning ERP or back-end systems. If applications and business processes are not integrated, the customer will just see bad information more quickly. Interoperability across the enterprise is critical. Companies are synchronizing the front-office, back-office, supply chain, and customer-touching applications. Rather than needing ERP just for automating applications and business processes, ERP will be required to support a company's e-business strategy. AMR research predicts ERP vendors will continue to grow at a rate of about 30% per year from 2000 through 2005 by addressing the needs

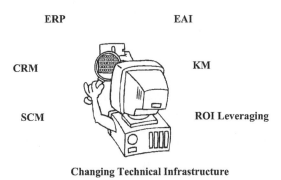

Business Application Trends

ERP   EAI

CRM   KM

SCM   ROI Leveraging

Changing Technical Infrastructure

Figure 1.8   Business Application Trends

of those companies that have work to do in this area.* Although this is half of their growth rate from 1995 to 2000, it is still a healthy growth rate. Examples of common ERP vendors include Oracle, SAP, PeopleSoft, and JDEdwards.

■ **Customer Relationship Management (CRM):** CRM software is used to optimize the efficiency of many areas of the enterprise by integrating areas such as sales, customer service, marketing, field support and service, and other customer-touching functions. CRM integrates people, process, and technology to maximize relationships with all customers including e-customers, distribution channel members, internal customers, and suppliers. CRM functionality includes:
  — Sales contact management, activity history
  — Proposal generation
  — Order entry and configuration
  — Sales management, forecasting, sales cycle analysis, sales metrics, territory alignment
  — Time management, calendar, scheduling, e-mail, task management
  — Telemarketing, telesales, call list development, auto dialing, scripting, call tracking
  — Customer service and support, incident assignment, escalation, tracking, reporting, problem resolution, warranty management
  — Field service, work-order dispatching, part management, preventive maintenance
  — Marketing, lead generation, lead tracking, campaign management, data mining
  — Executive information, business intelligence, reporting, balanced scorecards
■ CRM is enabled by the Internet, which allows:
  — Self servicing to reduce costs and increase service to the customer
  — Providing information any time anywhere, multi-modal access
  — Personalized services with one-to-one marketing
  — Automated lead generation and follow-up
  — Data synchronization for distributed processing
  — Enterprise portals
■ CRM had grown to a $50B industry by 1999, and is expected to grow to $125B by 2003 (Computer Economics). Industry analysts claim that the industry grew over 40% per year from 1995 to 2000 and

---

* Norris, Grant, Hurley, James R., Hartley, Kenneth M., Dunleavy, John R., and Balls, John, D., *E-Business and EPR*, John Wiley & Sons, New York, 2000, p. 182.

will continue that growth during the next 5 years. Many top CRM vendors (such as Siebel, SalesLogix, Saratoga, Clarify, Vantive, Pivotal, and Firstwave Technologies) are substantially increasing revenues each year. Major ERP vendors, such as Oracle, SAP Baan (who purchased Aurum), and PeopleSoft (who purchased Vantive), are beginning to push into the CRM market and also experience tremendous growth.

■ **Supply Chain Management (SCM):** Today, the majority of e-business transactions are business-to-business sales. Purchases for maintenance, repair, and operating (MRO) activities range from buying office furniture to consumable supplies. Organizations typically pay more than they realize to process these purchases with their paper-based systems. Computer Economics identified the typical cost for each of the paper-based orders in 1999 was $116, while the same purchase made on the Web cost less than $25. Furthermore, the cost of paper-based processing will continue to increase while Web procurement costs will decrease. Even more significant is the time wasted in processing purchases. The average organization required about 7 days in 1999 and 7.4 days in 2000 to move a purchase from request through approval. The same process done electronically took 2 days and 1.5 days in 1999 and 2000, respectively.

■ **Enterprise Application Integration (EAI):** It is becoming critical to synchronize front-office, back-office, and supply chain activities to attract and retain customers, fulfill demand, and improve cycle times and profits. Processes and information must be integrated worldwide. This integration can be difficult with different ERP systems within a company or for companies with an acquisition strategy, continually acquiring entities with differing ERP systems. A vendor's lack of integration is evident when it is unable to immediately provide an available-to-promise date for delivery of an item. EAI technology makes the integration of differing systems possible.

■ **Changing Technical Infrastructure:** Security, continuous availability, and scalability requirements are driving a new technical architecture. The new architecture includes business component architecture, object orientation, smaller footprints, and interoperability (with defined Application Program Interfaces). Technical trends such as hand-held devices and remote devices provide any time anywhere access. Application Service Providers (ASPs) are also utilized when it may be more feasible to obtain external services.

■ **Knowledge Management (KM):** Analytical applications with canned data marts, data warehouses, data mining (looking for patterns and relationships in data), and artificial intelligence are increasing in acceptance and utilization as means to obtain more value from the increasing volumes of data that are collected. Tools to analyze the content and context of documents and generate visual maps to navigate through the data are valuable. Push technologies that automatically deliver information to a user based on a profile help manage a distributed environment.

■ **Return on Investment (ROI) Applications:** Companies are developing applications on both the Internet and Intranet to increase sales and improve the return on investment. Photo-based organization charts, departmental news, company procedures, and office maps are nice but they do not help pay for the company Intranet. Companies are starting to look outside company bounds to establish a return on their Intranets. Other companies may be willing to pay a significant amount of money (or discounts) to be positioned on a company Intranet. These relationships can be beneficial to all the companies as well as to the employees. In an Intranet promotional partnership, the company receives discounts or payment in exchange for the ability to market goods and services to employees through the Intranet, for example, money management services, financial and housing programs, health and wellness programs, travel services, banking services, office supplies, products, or books. Companies are also looking at how they can obtain a profit from their Internet sites. Some companies are charging for content and information by selling information and reports or charging a monthly fee for providing access to certain information.

■ **Communication Applications:** Web conferencing, Web broadcasting, Web-based training, and groupware enable one-to-one, one-to-many, and many-to-many communication. Companies are integrating this powerful two-way communication vehicle into their Internet functionality.

It is critical to acknowledge these business application trends and determine their possible impact on enabling a business strategy of the future.

TECHNOLOGY TRENDS

There are many advances in technology that enable the e-business era and application changes discussed above. There are technology changes in all areas of the infrastructure, including the network communications and servers as well as the desktop and peripherals:

■ **Network communications:** Connectivity is increasing. Everything is electronically connected to everything else. An example is the Cadillac

On-Star program (www.cadillac.com) that relays an electronic message to a control center to dispatch assistance when an airbag is inflated. Numerous telecommunications advances, such as satellite communications and improved fiber optics, enable increased connectivity. There has been a melding of voice, data, and video. New communications architecture alternatives include point-to-point tunnel protocols (PPTP) and layer two tunneling protocol (L2TP) that allows entrance to the corporate network through firewalls via the Internet or semi-private networks. There is an increased use and reliance on the Internet as a backbone.

■ **Servers:** With improved efficiencies in servers, the total cost of processing a business transaction continues to decrease. Throughout server architecture, there is increased interoperability and communication among diverse platforms. Object-oriented programming (OOP) continues to improve. Although object programming may not have come on as strong or successful as many predicted, with interoperability increasing, solutions can be integrated more so than in the past. Also with increased interoperability, there is a convergence of the infrastructure and an increased importance and availability of middleware. Distributed computing is enabled by improved data synchronization ability and enterprise synchronization with personal database and multiple database servers. There has also been an increased use of Java, HTML, XML, and other Web development and thin-client technologies to support n-tier architecture. Graphics, video, and sound capabilities have improved due to compression algorithms, larger storage devices, and improved multimedia technology. Executive information systems provide users with increased power to obtain information. Application service providers are increasing in popularity to support the growing requirements.

■ **Desktop and peripherals:** Computer chips are becoming smaller and more powerful. They are embedded into nearly everything, making processing ubiquitous. Wireless technology provides information everywhere. Cellular and other mobile technologies allow sending and receiving of data anywhere. Natural and easy-to-use interfaces enable more people to use technology, with features such as voice recognition. There is an increase in multi-modal access, hand-held, and personal digital assistant (PDA) devices to provide the ability to access information any time and anywhere. Computer and telephone integration, pen-based computers, and other mobile devices such as bar coding and smart cards improve the entry and transmission of information. Security is improving through the use of encryption, biometric, and other measures such as iris, retina, and fingerprint recognition.

The challenge for an organization is understanding what the various trends in business, business applications, and technology mean to the business and identifying emerging opportunities due to the changes and trends. Companies must also learn to react quickly and take advantage of opportunities before the environment changes.

BARRIERS TO E-BUSINESS

Many companies experience barriers to moving to an e-business model. This is not as simple as building a Web site or installing packaged software applications. It means fundamentally changing how the business processes function.

Some of the barriers are shown in Figure 1.9. They may include:

- **Channel market conflict:** One large manufacturer went quickly into the e-business era and launched the capability for consumers to purchase its product over the Internet. Its previous channel had been solely through distributors. When the distributors were informed of the company's new endeavor, they were very unhappy and threatened to stop distributing the company's product. The company almost lost its entire core business by failing to understand the full impact of its new Internet endeavor. It quickly removed its newfound Internet functionality.

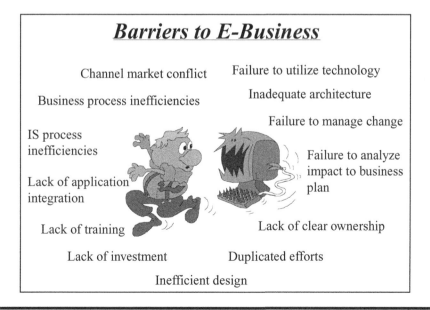

Figure 1.9   Barriers to E-Business

■ **Business process inefficiencies:** A total of 26% of respondents in the A.T. Kearney survey of 251 global CEOs from 26 countries across 10 industry segments identified organizational structure and existing business processes as the top challenges to implementing e-business.* The web is an excellent vehicle to gain new customers and establish close relationships, but it is also a great place to lose customers. Although many executives would find it totally unacceptable to have their phone lines down for 10 seconds, their internal processes may take days for a customer to get an e-mail reply. A study by Jupiter Communications LLC (www.jup.com) found that 42% of top sites surveyed failed to provide adequate customer services by taking longer than 5 days to reply to e-mail inquiries, not replying at all, or not being accessible by e-mail. Business processes must be designed to respond quickly to customers. Once a customer is disappointed by slow response, he or she is unlikely to try again. This customer is probably lost for good.

■ **Information systems process inefficiencies:** When companies go into e-business, they often forget to analyze the impact on their information systems processes. To function properly in an e-business world, the information systems processes may require radical changes. Examples include:

— Perhaps it was very acceptable in the past to resolve a PC problem logged at the HELP desk in an average of 2 hours. In an e-business environment, 2 hours to resolve an issue with the Web site could kill a company or impact the stock price. The problem management process is only one of many processes that may need to be redesigned.

— The capacity and storage management process may not be set up to handle the quickly scalable demands of the Internet world. Victoria's Secret (www.victoriassecret.com) is just one of many companies that learned the importance of this when it launched its first online style show. It was surprised that the number of viewers caused its system to crash. Victoria's Secret learned from that experience and added load-balancing and other preventive measures. The company now ranks high on the list of Web sites based on performance.

— The systems development process must be able to modify systems quickly to accomodate the needs of the customer and business.

— The change management process must be tighter than ever to ensure modifications do not impact system availability. Information

---

* A.T. Kearney, "Intellectual Capital," http://www.atkearney.com/ATK/Publications/ ic_detail/1,1071,1369,00.html.

systems processes are addressed in depth in *A Practical Guide to Information Systems Process Improvement* published by St. Lucie Press (2001).

■ **Lack of application integration:** If business applications are not integrated, the Internet is nothing more than a super fax machine. Information cannot be fragmented, inaccurate, or not timely for Internet applications to function properly. Pieces of information cannot be stored in manual files or islands of Excel spreadsheets. Applications on the front end and back end must be integrated to provide accurate delivery and availability of information. Applications should be designed for single-source data entry from point of origin. If information is not integrated, it is immediately obvious to the customer. For example, an order for drapes and valance from a company resulted in the acceptance of an online order. A day later (after some batch processing), an e-mail confirmation (from the system that manages the production of the valance) sent to the customer stated that the order was backordered. A few hours later (from the system that manages the production of the drapes), an e-mail confirmation was sent to the customer stating the order was shipped. After waiting a week for delivery, the customer opened the shipment, which included only the drapes with a message that the valance was no longer manufactured. The transaction resulted in a very unhappy (and lost) customer who returned the order.

■ **Lack of training:** When implementing e-business, training cannot be underestimated. In many cases, business processes and the entire jobs of individuals may change. Individuals may not be skilled in the new technology and fail to meet job expectations. Technical people may need to be trained in entirely new languages and tools.

■ **Lack of investment:** E-enabling an enterprise is not for the faint hearted. It is a large effort that requires financial and human investment throughout the course. Proper funds and resources must be allocated to develop and maintain the functionality, Web site, and processes. Forrester Research Inc. estimates a basic site costs $1.5M and the most sophisticated of sites more than $15M.* Forrester also states that a business can count on spending another $700K/year to maintain a basic site and up to $4M/year to run a high-end site. The majority of the costs are labor, including programmers, graphic designers, content creators, and business analysts.

---

* From a Forrester Research Inc. report, "What Business Sites Cost," cited in Kalin, Sari, "It's Not Easy Being B2B," *CIO Web Business*, Section 2, October 1, 1999.

■ **Inefficient design from customer vantage point:** Using the Internet is appealing largely because of the immediate gratification it promises. Visitors want to be able to get to a Web site, make a decision, obtain information, or solve a problem fast. Inability to find information is worse than not having the information at all, because the result is a frustrated customer with a question rather than just a customer with a question. Statistics indicate that it is only a matter of seconds before visitors give up a search and move to another site if they are unable to locate the information they need. Competitors are only a click away. The Web site design must be organized and easy to navigate for the customer. It is important to consider the total customer interactive requirements, rather than just viewing the site as an electronic brochure. Make sure the site turns up at the top of search lists, or the potential customer may never reach the site.

■ **Decentralized and duplicated efforts:** Internet development often occurs in independent projects across an organization as the power of the technology is realized by business units. Duplicate efforts may occur throughout the company, particularly if the Information Systems department is not proactive in addressing the technology and how the company will be utilizing it. Different divisions or geographic areas may develop overlapping or even conflicting information and functionality. A strategic e-business plan is critical to bring the efforts of the entire enterprise together to ensure a consistent direction.

■ **Lack of clear accountability or ownership:** If there are duplicate Internet efforts within the company, it may be unclear who has final authority and responsibility. Some companies may consider this final authority to be a technical person or the Chief Information Officer/ Vice President of Information Systems. However, e-business is not solely a technical endeavor; instead, it should be viewed as a critical business initiative with a key leader or officer from the business as the sponsor.

■ **Failure to analyze the impact to the business plan:** Companies that just begin Internet projects without planning may find themselves with a hodgepodge of unrelated functionality that may not provide the business with a competitive advantage. Worse yet, the Internet may have a substantial negative effect on the business that may go undetected and significantly impact the business. A company may be redirecting assets to Internet initiatives without realizing that its entire business model must change. To do e-business properly, a company must go back to the basics and analyze the impact of the Internet on the business plan.

- **Failure to manage change:** E-business can have a significant impact on the entire business and business processes. E-business often fails because the company fails to recognize and manage the human and cultural components of change. Management must help individuals by guiding them through the various stages of change. Communication at all levels within the organization is essential during this period of change.
- **Inadequate architecture:** The technical infrastructure must be continually assessed to ensure that it is sufficient. Management tools must monitor performance and predict future loads. Technical designs need to address performance and availability requirements to ensure single points of failure and redundancy are addressed properly. Security concerns must continually be addressed.
- **Failure to utilize technology:** Each day, new technologies are being developed that enhance Internet capabilities. If a business does not continually evaluate the viability of these technologies, it may lose benefits. For example, don't rely on customers finding the Web site on their own; use e-mail to aggressively market the company and direct them to the site. Ensure the Web site is coming up on the top of appropriate searches. Use e-mail to forge an ongoing customer relationship and communication. Track where customers are going and their interests. I recently experienced a very impressive use of technology when I attended a symposium of CRM packages. After visiting various booths and viewing countless demonstrations, upon returning to my room, I received e-mail messages from several vendors, thanking me for stopping by and directing me to their sites. One vendor even tracked my activities on his site. The company went on to send me a message acknowledging that I had visited its booth and visited its Web site, and based on the pages that I went to on its Web site, asked if I would be interested in additional information about a specific topic. That was a vendor that truly practiced what it preached! To create a truly responsive site, the processes must be automated and quick to respond. As site traffic increases, manual processes will be unable to keep up. Deploy automation that is scalable with the demands. Using the proper tools and automation can make the difference between online success and online failure.

LESSONS LEARNED

Many lessons can be learned from other companies that have blazed the e-business path. We can be thankful to those companies that have taken the risk, tried it, and succeeded or failed, as other organizations can learn from their experiences. Without their courageous attempts, we would not be challenged to move forward. Some lessons that companies have learned include:

■ **E-business exposes weaknesses to the world:** The only thing worse than no e-business presence is a bad e-business presence. A company that had a bad process before e-business will have this inefficient or ineffective process highlighted and magnified to the world after implementation of e-business. Systems now directly impact the customer. For example, in the past, a customer service agent could mask system inadequacies, but now customers directly enter the order. Information must be automated and integrated. There must be one single global view of the customer rather than disparate pieces of customer interaction information.

■ **There are no boundaries:** E-business brings together diverse interests. In the past, businesses could operate in silos of functional departments, plans, sales territories, countries, cultures, and languages. With e-business, the design needs to stand the test of crossing all the barriers. Components of the entire global business must share a common language, rules, goals, and commitment.

■ **E-business challenges the business strategy:** Technology is becoming a critical enabling component to the business direction. E-business requires companies to rethink the business plan and the information systems strategic plan. It may impact the basics such as the mission, value chain, and business objectives. To be successful, companies must identify what they do well as businesses and determine how they can transfer these assets or maximize them with Internet technologies. Markets and industries can be quickly impacted by Internet initiatives. Companies need to take leading roles with their e-business directions. The Internet can eliminate switching costs. An alternative is just a click away. Boundaries in e-business markets are not clearly defined, as competitors can enter from indirect ways or even from other markets. Companies can use technologies, relationships, and information flows to disrupt value chains and assume new positions. To be successful, companies must continually evaluate the impact of the Internet and technology on their direction, goals, and industry.

■ **Need to design from the customer viewpoint:** There has been an attitude shift to give the customers what they want, when they want it, and how they want it. Companies that are leaders are customer-led companies. They focus on groups of individuals rather than on products or services. All customer points of interaction must be considered. Focus on what the customer wants, not what the company wants to market. Focus on how the customer views the company and on customer interactions with the company.

- **Need to plan:** To be successful, a company must plan its e-business strategy. Properly executed e-business requires an alignment of the business vision and business strategy, efficient cross-functional business processes, efficient information systems processes, integrated application framework, and a solid information systems technical infrastructure. E-business requires a new skill set and new culture. Companies must thoroughly understand the financials of the e-business strategy. E-business can be an endless pit of expenditures without a return on investment if not planned properly. The Gartner Group predicts that, by the end of 2001, over 70% of companies will have failed to plan a coherent approach to e-business, leading to a significant loss of competitiveness.*
- **Need to act now:** Although we are all still learning about the new e-business frontier, companies can no longer continue to do only what made them successful in the past. All companies must review and adjust their business models before it is too late and they fall behind the competition. Companies cannot afford to be complacent. They must transform into lean and agile companies that anticipate and quickly react to change. E-business is a continuous process. The only certainty is uncertainty. Companies must have a strategy, make short-term plans, execute rapidly, learn, and modify their approaches. The strategy must continually evolve as technology and market changes occur.

The world has started to see Internet failures resulting from companies dashing into the e-business world without realizing the full impact to their businesses. Newspapers and magazines are filled with stories about companies that have suffered or even died because of their e-business mistakes. Consider the following examples:

- A store had a large marketing effort for its new e-business functionality. It was astounded by the large number of visitors. The site crashed in a matter of minutes. Results of this lack of planning were angry customers, bad publicity, and negative impact to store stock.
- A food manufacturer advertised a valuable coupon available on its Internet site. The coupon provided had already expired, which resulted in a flood of calls to the customer support desk. The support desk crashed under the volume. The result was angry customers.
- A clothing manufacturer had an online store that allowed customers to place orders. However, the orders were lost because the

---

* Gartner Group Interactive Home, September 15, 1999, www.gartner.com.

communication link between the company and the ISP had gone down.

■ An aviation parts distributor launched a new Web-based order-entry system. The sales reps feared their jobs were at stake and badmouthed the site to customers, telling them not to use it. The sales reps viewed the customer service that they were personally providing the customers as a competitive advantage. The site was not used.

■ A leading online company underestimated traffic and did not have the capacity to handle the volume. On Thanksgiving weekend, the site saw a 50% increase in sales over the previous weekend. It took an hour for the ISP host to reroute the load. As a result of lost orders and unhappy customers, the stock plummeted.

■ A leading department store underestimated online traffic; following a splashy launch, the site crashed and remained unoperational for about 3 weeks.

■ A catalog retailer's value dropped 25% because the retailer failed to align Internet sales with its existing catalog strategies.

Many of these issues occurred in the execution, and the majority could have been avoided through proper planning. To do e-business properly, a business must go back to the basics of its business plan and information systems plan. E-business implemented properly can be a tremendous success and positively impact the company. Giga Information Group estimates that e-commerce projects saved U.S. businesses more than $15B in 1998 and could save as much as $600B by 2002.* These savings are realized in areas such as order handling, marketing communications, supply chain management, and procurement. One company that has implemented many of these techniques and principles utilizing Internet and e-business technology since 1994 is Cisco Systems, Inc. Cisco has 24,000 employees and has grown by acquisition of more than 50 companies since 1993. Cisco has changed its entire company culture to be Web-centric with virtually all information and processes conducted on the Web. The Internet is ubiquitous, a part of everything Cisco does. Cisco is driven by its core competencies as it does what it does best and outsources the rest. Its entire business is re-evaluated every 6 months. Some of its results are:

■ 83% of all customer inquiries are handled on the Web
■ 25% increase in customer satisfaction

---

* Giga Information Group quoted in "A Penny Saved," *CIO Web Business*, Section 2, October 1, 1999, p. 24.

- An estimated financial benefit of $825M in FY'99 resulting from Internet applications
- Decrease in order error rate from 35% to less than 1%
- 87% of orders are placed online
- $14.9B in annual transactions via e-commerce
- ISO training was completed in 5 weeks for $16K with a 93% pass rate; the classroom costs would have been $1.4M over 4 months
- 55% of product fulfillment by supply partners
- 45% reduction in supply chain inventory
- 25% faster new product development time
- Employee travel expenses paid within 48 hours by wiring to the bank
- Less than 3% employee turnover
- Financial worldwide close reduced from 14 days to within an hour
- Accounts receivable cost per invoice went from 97 cents in 1997 to 65 cents in 1999
- Payroll cost per paycheck went from $7.03 in 1997 to $4.20 in 1999
- Accounts payable headcount per $100M went from 1.1 in 1997 to .6 in 1999
- Highest industry productivity—which is double its nearest competitor—with $690K sales per employee

In addition to Cisco, other examples of companies using e-business to improve their competitive position include:

- GE (www.ge.com) conducts purchasing through its Trading Process Network Extranet. In the first year, GE achieved average savings of 20% on materials sourced and reduced cycle times by 50%.
- Results from companies such as GE and 3Com indicate an average reduction in information request processing from $45 to $1.50 per order by using the Internet to field requests for product prices, availability, and order status.
- Firms such as Fisher Scientific and 3M have cut order processing time in half by using the Internet to accept orders and interface into legacy systems.
- Ford Motor Company (www.ford.com) moved $16B in purchases from over 3,000 suppliers to the Internet. Ford integrated the design and engineering into the supply chain and saved $1K per vehicle and reduced design-cycle time by 33%, to 2 years.
- Lands' End (www.landsend.com) implemented click-to-talk direct link to an agent to assist shoppers. It increased web sales from 4 to 10% of sales.
- Mindspring, an Internet service provider now called Earthlink (www.earthlink.net), built an online knowledge base of over 2,000

articles to help answer customer questions without human interven-
tion. This e-service implementation paid for itself in 1 month.

■ PictureTel (www.picturetel.com) is a provider of teleconferencing
solutions. Its cost per support call was approximately $60, but by
implementing e-service, it was able to reduce call volume by 32%.

■ Dell (www.dell.com) computer developed "Dell Online" in 1996 for
e-commerce. Dell generates over $14M in e-commerce sales per day,
with business-to-business sales accounting for 70% of its Web revenue. The products purchased online provide a 30% higher profit
margin than those purchased through traditional methods.

■ Wells Fargo has halved the cost per transaction while increasing the
average balance per customer through online service.

■ General Mills utilized the Internet to automate the supply chain,
realizing $700K savings in 3 months with one partner. With col-
laboration of its other 19 partners, it plans to cut 6%, or $24M from
its annual shipping costs.

There are many examples of how e-business can improve each stage
in the process of delivering value for companies, including:

■ **Marketing:** Builds and manages the worldwide company image,
manages and qualifies leads, keeps the company abreast of customer needs, and generates customer interest. The more useful a
site is, the more positively prospects will view the company. Sites
that attract and retain visitors with interesting and up-to-date information are essentially increasing advertising with minimal to no
additional investment. The Internet expands the available market
and streamlines the sales cycle.

■ **Order management:** Manages the process from quote to order,
shortens the customer decision time, assists in the acquisition process,
and helps companies understand customer behavior, thus increasing
customer retention and loyalty.

■ **Fulfillment:** Provides instant feedback and information through all
the channels. Improves communication, reduces inventory and cycle
times. Reduces overall costs. Provides monitoring of utilization of
products and services. Products are tracked through shipping and the
fulfillment process.

■ **Service:** Provides immediate customer support and service, improves
customer satisfaction, speeds transactions, and lowers the cost of support. When customers can help themselves on a Web site rather than
calling customer service, savings can range from $10 to $50 or more
per incident. By adding additional customer-driven content, the number
of customers who can help themselves also increases, dramatically

reducing overall customer support costs. By helping themselves, customers also get answers more quickly, resulting in increased satisfaction.

IMPORTANCE OF PLANNING

Although the path to e-business has barriers and challenges, as shown above, many companies have surmounted the challenges and experienced tremendous success. A critical component to success is a good plan. As shown in Figure 1.10, the familiar saying, "failing to plan is planning to fail," is definitely true for the e-business journey.

The e-business journey must begin with a solid, recently updated business plan that takes into consideration the impact of the Internet. The business plan, in turn, should drive the information systems plan, which prioritizes and drives the individual e-business initiatives that are finally implemented. Although this may seem like a basic principle, too many companies begin by implementing random shots at e-business efforts. As shown in Figure 1.11, the plan should provide a guiding light to ensure that both the business and the technology end up at the same destination.

An e-business strategic plan can answer many questions, including:

- What are the current technology trends and how can they best be utilized for the business?
- What is the status of the current e-business environment? What are the strengths, areas of improvement and risk?
- What additional business opportunities exist because of the Internet? What impact does the Internet have on the business?

Figure 1.10   Failing to Plan

A Strategic Plan Provides a Guiding Light

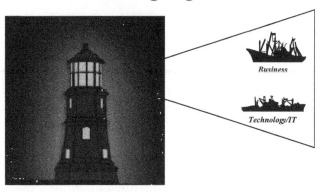

Figure 1.11   A Plan Provides a Guiding Light

- How are competitors utilizing the Internet?
- How will e-business impact existing distribution channels?
- What changes and risks are there in the industry and value chain?
- How can the company provide value in the new economy?
- How can the company utilize Internet technology to provide a competitive advantage in the marketplace?
- Does the company have the right people, skill set, and organization to effectively become an e-enabled organization?
- How must the business processes change to efficiently handle e-business?
- Does the business have the right technical infrastructure to support e-business?
- How do the information systems processes need to change to meet the new business requirements?
- What e-business opportunities should be pursued?
- What are the best e-business projects and priorities?
- What is the business case and justification for doing e-business?
- What is the roadmap for implementing the necessary e-business functionality?
- How will the success of Internet projects and investments be measured?
- What should be the entrance strategy into e-business?

By completing the strategy before implementing individual e-business efforts, the company will:

- Ensure funds and resources are allocated correctly
- Maintain focus on the business goals and direction
- Ensure business processes are e-enabled
- Ensure the technical infrastructure can handle the e-business direction
- Obtain a competitive advantage in the market place
- Enable new market channels, penetrate into new markets, or supplement channel activities
- Ensure it has fully reviewed the impact of the Internet and other technologies on the business and industry
- Facilitate communication throughout the business
- Establish a common vision and direction
- Help balance the level of ambition, potential benefits, tolerance for risk, and willingness to invest

KEY POINTS TO REMEMBER

- The Internet has had a significant impact on our organizations and has increased the importance of technology to the success of businesses.
- To be successful, re-invent the business model with the new technology as the Internet enables business in entirely new ways. E-business places new requirements on companies today.
- E-business is utilizing Internet technologies to improve and integrate people, processes, and technology. E-business encompasses the entire business model with customers, suppliers, partners, employees, and the company. Successful companies will e-enable their entire enterprises so that Internet technologies are tightly integrated into all the core business processes.
- It is important for companies to understand the trends in business, business applications, and technology to identify opportunities or risks that may emerge. The new economy is significantly different from the past economy. What made companies successful in the past may not necessarily carry them into the future.
- Although there are barriers and obstacles to implementing e-business, many companies have implemented e-business successfully and realized significant benefits.
- Developing a thorough e-business strategy and a plan that is tied to the business plan is critical to the success of e-business projects and initiatives.

NOTES FOR MY E-BUSINESS EFFORT

2

E-BUSINESS PLANNING OVERVIEW

"By failing to prepare you are preparing to fail."

Benjamin Franklin

PLANNING PRINCIPLES

How can an organization achieve the goal of becoming an e-enabled enterprise that utilizes e-business for a competitive advantage in the marketplace? There are always many different methodologies or ways to accomplish a goal. This book presents one way that works. Feel free to take the methodology and modify it to fit your particular needs and company, as all environments have slightly different needs. The key is to utilize some methodology or process to plan the e-business journey. Far too many organizations take the "Ready, Fire, Aim" approach to e-business and then wonder why they are unsuccessful or spend all their time catching up to competition, never really gaining a competitive edge. Actually, as stated by Mika Yamamoto Krammer, a Gartner Group senior analyst, this is really a "Ready! Fire! Duck! Clean Up!" mode.*

The old and lengthy business planning models will not work in the new environment. A 24- to 36-month planning cycle is neither realistic nor affordable. Instead, an iterative process is necessary that allows changing to multiple planned and quick "Ready, Aim, Fire" sequences. This means establishing a new business model, planning, and implementing in a very

---

* "Quote of the Week," *Information Week*, March 12, 2001, p. 17, www.information-week.com.

Integrated Design

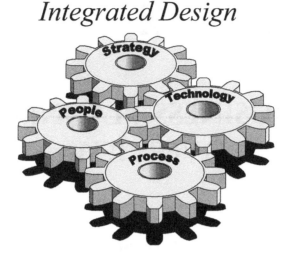

Figure 2.1   Integrated Design

short cycle time (i.e., 3 to 6 months). In today's quickly changing environment, this shortened planning cycle can be accomplished only by an agile organization with an in-depth understanding of customers, business, market, and industry. Take advantage of the strengths of the business and mold it into what customers want it to be. The methodology presented here provides one way to make the transformation successful.

Before presenting the methodology for planning the e-business environment, let us review the seven key principles upon which the methodology is based.

First Principle

There are various components to e-business, including the business strategy, the organization or people, and the processes, as well as the technology. All of these components are necessary for e-business success. As Figure 2.1 shows, these components must be integrated and work in concert. Often, when a company addresses e-business, it focuses solely on the technology aspects and ignores other critical components. The following is a brief description of each of the necessary components:

■ **Strategy:** For a company to be successful at e-business, it must have a solid and thorough business plan in addition to an e-business strategy. The business plan must be up to date and consider the changes in the market as well as customer expectations. The strategy establishes the vision of where the company wants to be and how the technology will help the company achieve the vision.

▪ **People:** E-business may require completely new people, new skills, and different organizational structures in both the business areas as well as the Information Systems areas. People must be properly trained, managed, allocated, and motivated.

▪ **Processes:** E-business may require the creation of new processes or the modification of existing processes in both the business and information systems organization. Processes may require changes to increase the speed of doing business. Information systems processes may need to change to meet availability and speed requirements. For example, is the problem management process fast enough? Is the availability high enough? Are current security controls sufficient? Is change control process complete enough?

▪ **Technology:** The technology includes both the business applications and the technical infrastructure. To support e-business, existing business applications may require changes or integration. Entirely new business applications may also be necessary to meet the e-business requirements. Which business applications need to be e-enabled? Implementing e-business may also require new or changed technology platform components such as hardware and network equipment. For example, is there sufficient hardware, redundancy with no single points of failure, and is it scalable to grow with the business?

Second Principle

As Figure 2.2 shows, business requirements and strategy, industry direction, key design principles, and anchor points all influence the e-business strategy. Anchor points are major investments and core infrastructure items upon which the current environment is based. An example of an anchor point is that all the business applications may be written on the mainframe. Although it may be desirable to move off the mainframe for various reasons, it probably cannot happen overnight. Typically, existing organizations cannot afford to rebuild their technical environment in one step and must plan the evolution of key components of their current environment.

Third Principle

The planning process is as important as the plan itself. The questions asked are as important as the answers obtained. Communication and involvement from all areas of the business is critical. The effort must be owned by the

Plan Components

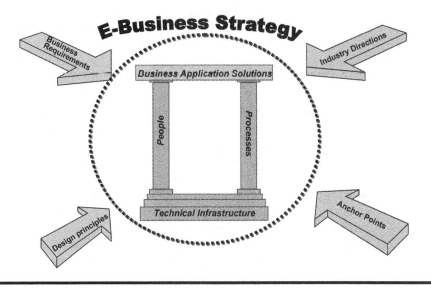

Figure 2.2   Plan Components

business, as it is a business project. I do not recommend hiring someone to develop a plan in isolation; it needs to be a joint effort with the consultant, key business executives, and information systems personnel. Although consultants can be very helpful in providing a focus, processing and facilitating the effort, internal resources know the business, industry, customers, and goals. In order to have a plan that can be implemented successfully, build the commitment and ownership through the planning process. For individuals to be supportive, it is essential that they feel they have input into the process. Obtain input by using group working sessions or interviews. Through this involvement, you can obtain valuable input and also improve the odds of successfully implementing the plan.

Fourth Principle

The business plan must drive the e-business strategy and technology strategy. The e-business strategy must be a part of and support the overall business strategy and plan. Although this seems like a very basic principle, too many companies attempt to implement e-business projects without having solid business plans in place. It is critical to think through the business model and the impact of the Internet before implementing

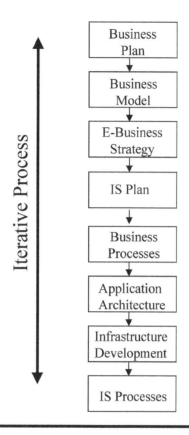

Figure 2.3   Business Plan Drives the Process

individual projects and initiatives. Without this consideration, the organization might find that it is spending a lot of money solving the wrong problem. If a formal business plan does not exist, ask the questions of a business planning process as part of the e-business strategy development. As Figure 2.3 shows, the business plan is the driver for the business model, e-business strategy, and information systems plan. Only then can the business processes, application architecture, technical infrastructure, and information systems processes be designed. This is an iterative process as each of these components may impact the others.

Fifth Principle

The level of detail for the e-business strategy planning process is critical. It is necessary to outline and analyze the strategy in sufficient detail, as the issues, difficulties, and problems are often found in the detail. Some people think that a business plan or a strategy is a few lofty mission statements that mean little to the organization. Planning, done right, is much more than that. Planning translates the organizational goals into strategies, day-to-day projects and tasks that can be implemented. This is true for business planning as well as e-business planning. It is far better to spend the time to fully develop the strategy rather than invest a lot of money and stumble in the marketplace.

Sixth Principle

Design the e-business strategy from the outside in. In other words, design the e-business strategy from the customer vantage point. A customer-centric e-business model drives value across the enterprise. Sell products and services in a manner that makes the customer want to buy. This principle is the single largest difference between the methodology presented in this book and traditional business planning methodologies. Typically, planning processes start with where is the company today, where does it want to be, what is the gap, and how does it get there. Traditional planning methods are focused from the inside out, looking at what the company wants to accomplish. In the new economy, with the customer as the driver, it is necessary for this view to change. Control is moving away from businesses and into the hands of customers. This is a major change from how planning is typically done in organizations today. This methodology starts with identifying who are the current and future customers and what do they want from the business, rather than what management wants the business to accomplish. This perspective may seem like a minor change, but it is a tremendous change to typical processes and thinking. Rather than prioritizing projects and action items based on return on investment or internal goals, have customers prioritize what is important to them. Rather than measuring the success of e-business ventures by sales generated, perhaps customer satisfaction may be a more accurate metric. If the customer is satisfied, it follows that sales will increase. This principle is the opposite of the "build it and they will come" mentality taken by many of the recent dot com start-ups that either quickly went out of business or never saw a profit. Focus on the customer and keep customer needs in the forefront, but do not dismiss the fundamental management principles of profit and loss to manage the business. Throughout the planning process, ask questions from the customer's perspective.

It is critical to make the company easy to do business with. As an experiment, try doing business with your company. You might be surprised to find out how difficult it is. The best way to be easy to do business with is to design processes from the customer perspective. Using technology that delivers personalized service, self-service, and a sense of community

E-Business is an Evolving Process

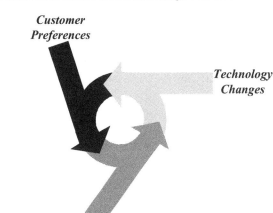

Figure 2.4   E-Business is an Evolving Process

can foster customer loyalty and actually make it difficult for customers to switch to alternatives.

Seventh Principle

As Figure 2.4 shows, e-business planning must be an iterative process. In today's fast moving and changing world, you cannot simply create a strategy and plan, and then ignore technology advances and changes in customer preferences. The speed at which the company reacts to marketplace changes and the flexibility it has to incorporate changes is the key to success. Business planning, e-business planning, and information systems planning need to become processes that are integrated in core management processes rather than occasional events. When planning, don't try for a perfect solution. Set priorities within the strategy and work on the most critical items first. Continue re-evaluating and modifying the strategy during the process.

An e-business plan must be done:

- Quickly
- In a planned and logical fashion
- Without negatively impacting the core business
- As part of business planning and information systems planning process
- With key business management involvement
- By starting small, thinking big, and going fast!

STRATEGY DEFINITION

What is an e-business strategy and plan? It is a roadmap used to implement an idea or direction. It takes into account where the business is today and where it wants to be. Most importantly, however, it takes into account what the customers want the business to become.

Exhibit 2.1 outlines a sample table of contents for an e-business plan. Each component in the sample table of contents is critical and serves an important purpose. The following is an overview of the sections of the deliverable presented in this methodology. In the remainder of this book, each of these sections will be explained in more detail.

- ■ **Executive summary:** One to two pages summarizing each section of the plan.
- ■ **Introduction:** Outlines the purpose of the plan document, the process utilized for the initial development as well as the ongoing maintenance. It also identifies the individuals involved in e-business and outlines their specific responsibilities.
- ■ **Trends:** Outlines the trends in the industry that impact the organization. This includes business trends, business application, and technical trends.
- ■ **Current situation:** Outlines the current status of the Intranet, Internet, and Extranet environments for the company. For each environment, include the business functionality currently provided, the technical environment, the people supporting it with their responsibilities, and the processes supporting the environment. This section includes the facts of the current environments, without editorials or analysis of the issues.
- ■ **Situation analysis:** Provides the analysis or opinions of the current situation outlined above. This section identifies the strengths and areas of improvement in the Intranet, Internet, and Extranet environments. Utilize a quantitative scorecard to communicate the status in various areas. All the stakeholders are identified as well as current and desired customers. Identify why they are customers, and what value the customers want the business to provide. Identify the decision process utilized by each stakeholder through the life of the relationship, beginning with deciding to do business with the company. Review and analyze the industry. Analyze and re-engineer the value chain. Analyze the business, including strengths, weaknesses, opportunities, and threats.
- ■ **Direction/strategy:** Define the value proposition or what value the company wants to provide to the stakeholders. A stakeholder is anyone who has an interest in the success or operation of the company, such as customers, shareholders, vendors, distributors, or

Exhibit 2.1 Sample Table of Contents for E-Business Plan

I. Executive Summary
II. Introduction
    A. Purpose of Document
    B. Planning Process
III. Trends
IV. Current Situation
    A. Intranet
    B. Internet
    C. Extranet
V. Situation Analysis
    A. Intranet
    B. Internet
    C. Extranet
    D. Scorecard
    E. Stakeholders
    F. Stakeholder Process
    G. Industry Analysis
    H. Value Chain
    I. Business Analysis
VI. Direction/Strategy
    A. Value Proposition
    B. Value Delivery Proposition
    C. Strategy
    D. Metrics
VII. Opportunities
    A. Customers
    B. Partners and Suppliers
    C. Public
    D. People/Employees
VIII. Competitive Situation
IX. E-Business Requirements
    A. Business Application
    B. Technical Infrastructure
    C. Information Systems Processes
    D. Business Processes
    E. People/Organization
X. Business Case
    A. Costs
    B. Benefits
    C. ROI
XI. Roadmap
XII. Appendix

the government. Define the tools or vehicle to deliver the value, the strategy and impact to the business plan, and the desired business impact, as well as how to measure success.

- **Opportunities:** Take each stakeholder and step in the decision-making process and ask how the company can achieve the value proposition in that step of the process. Answering this question will help identify various opportunities.

- **Competitive situation:** For each opportunity that was identified, review top competitors and rate how well they provide each particular functionality or opportunity. Then summarize the competitive situation and identify market opportunities and opportunities that will provide a competitive advantage.

- **E-business requirements:** Identify the specific action items and projects required to implement the e-business strategy and opportunities. You will need action items in the areas of business applications, technical infrastructure, people/organization, information systems processes, and business processes.

- **Business case:** Although it may be nice if companies would hand over large sums of money for information systems projects without asking for the benefits or return on investment, this is typically not the case (as it should be). Any major effort typically requires identifying all the costs, benefits, and return on investment.

- **Roadmap:** Prioritize and map the individual projects required to reach the end-point. Each project should be less than 3 months in duration, have a beginning and an end, with a specific deliverable and person responsible. Now that management knows where the company wants to be, it needs to communicate to the employees the steps to get there.

Initially, the table of contents suggested for an e-business plan may seem overwhelming, but it doesn't have to be a lengthy process. For a medium-size company, it could take 3 to 6 weeks. The first attempt at an e-business strategy can take longer because it requires a solid business plan, goals, and objectives. If the business goals and objectives have not been updated or clarified, the e-business strategy development may take a little longer because additional discussion of the business questions is required.

METHODOLOGY OVERVIEW

Now that you have an idea of what an e-business plan looks like and where we are headed, let's outline how to get there. As Figure 2.5 shows, there are eight phases to the methodology outlined in this book. The shape of the figure is meant to remind organizations to STOP and

Planning for E-Business Success

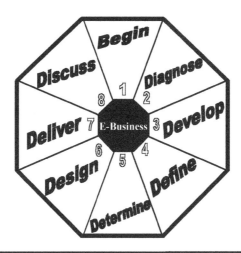

Figure 2.5   Methodology Phases

Figure 2.6   Stop and Plan

plan e-business ventures before implementing individual initiatives, as shown in Figure 2.6. The other item to note about the shape is that it is an iterative ongoing process. No sooner is the organization done, than the organization should start the process over again. The organization might go from one phase to the next and realize the need to go back and change something in a previous phase.

The phases include:

1. **Begin:** Begin by obtaining executive management support and a business sponsor. Identify the business purpose for completing an e-business plan and initiative. Identify the team of individuals that will be involved. Outline the planning process that will be used. Develop a communication plan outlining how members of the team and organization will be kept abreast of the activities. Finally, announce the project to the organization.
2. **Diagnose:** Diagnose trends and how they may impact the organization. Document the current environment and diagnose strengths and areas of improvement. Identify stakeholders and diagnose their process. Diagnose the industry and external impacts as well as the value chain. Diagnose the business strengths, weaknesses, opportunities, and threats.
3. **Develop:** Develop the value proposition as well as the value delivery proposition. Develop the e-business strategy and metrics to measure the success and progress of the strategy.
4. **Define:** Define specific opportunities as well as the competitive situation. Define priorities.
5. **Determine:** Determine the impact to the business application architecture, technical infrastructure, business processes, information systems processes, and people/organization. Determine the cost–benefit analysis as well as the roadmap to obtain the strategy. Obtain approval on the e-business plan to proceed with delivery of the plan.
6. **Design:** Design the look and feel required to implement the strategy and value proposition. Identify the navigation and screen design. Design the changes necessary to applications and security.
7. **Deliver:** Deliver the strategy and design by developing, testing, training, and implementing. Promote and market the e-business site and functionality.
8. **Discuss:** Discuss the results of the e-business venture by obtaining feedback and analyzing. Determine the necessary actions.

This list is meant to provide an overview of the process. Each chapter of this book will review each phase in detail and provide examples and questions to assist you. Figure 2.7 outlines the methodology.

Look again at the table of contents for the e-business plan. Exhibit 2.2 identifies the phases in which to prepare each section of the plan.

Note that the e-business plan is developed during Phases 1 through 5. Phases 6 through 8 are implementation steps. The main focus of this book is on the planning aspects in Phases 1 through 5, but general approaches are also provided for the implementation steps.

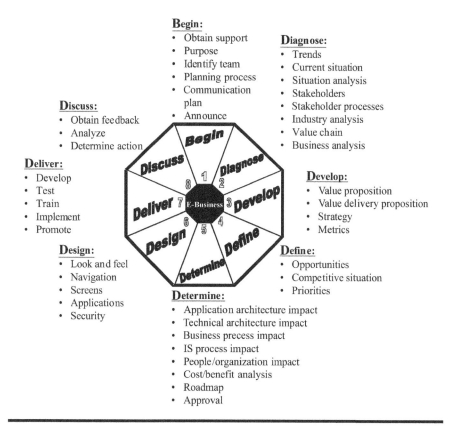

Begin:
- Obtain support
- Purpose
- Identify team
- Planning process
- Communication plan
- Announce

Diagnose:
- Trends
- Current situation
- Situation analysis
- Stakeholders
- Stakeholder processes
- Industry analysis
- Value chain
- Business analysis

Discuss:
- Obtain feedback
- Analyze
- Determine action

Deliver:
- Develop
- Test
- Train
- Implement
- Promote

Develop:
- Value proposition
- Value delivery proposition
- Strategy
- Metrics

Design:
- Look and feel
- Navigation
- Screens
- Applications
- Security

Define:
- Opportunities
- Competitive situation
- Priorities

Determine:
- Application architecture impact
- Technical architecture impact
- Business precess impact
- IS process impact
- People/organization impact
- Cost/benefit analysis
- Roadmap
- Approval

Figure 2.7   Methodology Overview

Exhibit 2.2   Phases of Plan Development

Table of Contents	When Developed
I. Executive Summary	**Phase 5—Determine**
II. Introduction	
A. Purpose of Document	**Phase 1—Begin**
B. Planning Process	**Phase 1—Begin**
III. Trends	**Phase 2—Diagnose**
IV. Current Situation	
A. Intranet	**Phase 2—Diagnose**
B. Internet	**Phase 2—Diagnose**
C. Extranet	**Phase 2—Diagnose**
V. Situation Analysis	
A. Intranet	**Phase 2—Diagnose**
B. Internet	**Phase 2—Diagnose**

(Continued)

Exhibit 2.2   Phases of Plan Development (continued)

	Table of Contents	*When Developed*
	C. Extranet	**Phase 2—Diagnose**
	D. Scorecard	**Phase 2—Diagnose**
	E. Stakeholders	**Phase 2—Diagnose**
	F. Stakeholder Process	**Phase 2—Diagnose**
	G. Industry Analysis	**Phase 2—Diagnose**
	H. Value Chain	**Phase 2—Diagnose**
	I. Business Analysis	**Phase 2—Diagnose**
VI.	Direction/Strategy	
	A. Value Proposition	**Phase 3—Develop**
	B. Value Delivery Proposition	**Phase 3—Develop**
	C. Strategy	**Phase 3—Develop**
	D. Metrics	**Phase 3—Develop**
VII.	Opportunities	
	A. Customers	**Phase 4—Define**
	B. Partners and Suppliers	**Phase 4—Define**
	C. Public	**Phase 4—Define**
	D. People/Employees	**Phase 4—Define**
VIII.	Competitive Situation	**Phase 4—Define**
IX.	E-Business Requirements	
	A. Business Application	**Phase 5—Determine**
	B. Technical Infrastructure	**Phase 5—Determine**
	C. Information Systems Processes	**Phase 5—Determine**
	D. Business Processes	**Phase 5—Determine**
	E. People/Organization	**Phase 5—Determine**
X.	Business Case	
	A. Costs	**Phase 5—Determine**
	B. Benefits	**Phase 5—Determine**
	C. ROI	**Phase 5—Determine**
XI.	Roadmap	**Phase 5—Determine**
XII.	Appendix	

KEY POINTS TO REMEMBER

■ The e-business strategy must be aligned with, and part of, the business strategy. E-business is not a technical endeavor, it is a business endeavor.

■ The components of the e-business strategy that must be considered include the business applications, the people/organization, the processes, and the technical infrastructure.

- The planning process, communication, and involvement are as important as the plan itself.
- Design the strategy from the outside in, from the customer vantage point.
- E-business planning is an iterative evolution. Speed and flexibility are essential. E-business planning is a process, not an event.
- The eight phases of the methodology presented in this book include begin, diagnose, develop, define, determine, design, deliver, and discuss.

NOTES FOR MY E-BUSINESS EFFORT

3

PHASE 1—BEGIN

"While we ponder when to begin it becomes too late to do."

Quintilian

As Figure 3.1 shows, the first phase of the e-business planning process is to **Begin**. As an e-business initiative will consume time, resources, and be of utmost importance to the business, it is paramount to begin the effort properly. During this phase, you will obtain management support and a business sponsor, identify the purpose of the e-business initiative, and identify the team and participants in the e-business effort. You will document the planning process to be utilized for the e-business project as well as define the communication plan that will keep the organization informed throughout the effort. Finally, you will announce this critical initiative to the organization. At the end of this phase, you will have completed the following sections in the e-business plan document:

- Purpose of Document
- Planning Process

Each of these sections is described in more detail, as follows.

OBTAIN SUPPORT

Executive management support is critical to the success of an e-business initiative. Without sufficient management support, it will be difficult to implement the effort successfully. Some questions to consider include:

- Is executive management ready to address the business planning and business model questions that will arise?

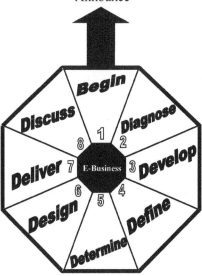

Begin:
- Obtain support
- Purpose
- Identify team
- Planning process
- Communication plan
- Announce

Figure 3.1 Phase 1, Begin

■ Is management willing to invest the time and money to see the project through implementation?

■ Is there a strong visionary business sponsor who is willing to be involved?

■ Does management need to be educated and enlightened on the impact of e-business?

■ Is executive management convinced of the impact that the Internet can have on the business?

Executive management may not instinctively appreciate the importance of e-business to its organization. It may be necessary to begin with executive management training, awareness, and discussions on trends in the industry. It can also be helpful to show management what competition is doing with e-business, or the results that other companies are experiencing as a result of e-business. In these discussions, it is important to translate what e-business can mean for the company and industry.

It is important to encourage executive management to take a strategic view of e-business. As with any new business and technology venture, there will be successes and failures or issues encountered. Particularly in the fast moving technology environment, failure is to be expected and actually encouraged as a way to make progress. The organization must learn from mistakes rather than punish individuals for taking the risks.

Executive management support for e-business is necessary to:

- Obtain the resources to work on the effort
- Provide funding as the effort is further defined
- Participate in developing the e-business strategy
- Participate in decisions that may impact the business direction
- Sponsor and approve the e-business projects
- Prioritize the e-business projects
- Make decisions on business process changes or organizational changes that may be necessary

Executive management provides a steering committee for the e-business initiatives. Typically, an executive management team may already exist in the form of a business management team or Information Systems Steering Committee. Ensure that e-business is on the agenda for this group during its regular meetings.

Identify a business sponsor for the e-business initiatives. This individual should take a key role in guiding e-business for the organization. The e-business sponsor should have the following traits and skills:

- Hold an executive-level position within the business (not Information Systems as e-business is a business issue, not a technical issue)
- Be influential within the organization
- Have the authority and responsibily to get resources, maintain involvement, make decisions, and ensure commitment
- Be a visionary
- Be passionate about e-business and possibilities with the Internet
- Have good communication skills
- Have the ability to make decisions
- Possess the ability to think outside of the box
- Have good knowledge of the business and industry
- Have good knowledge of the Internet and its capabilities

The role of the e-business executive sponsor is to:

- Assist with establishing the vision and strategy for e-business
- Assist in obtaining resources, making decisions, and obtaining commitment from all areas of the organization

■ Assist in communicating the e-business vision, strategy, and status to other areas of the organization

Depending on the size of the organization and the e-business involvement of the organization, being the executive sponsor could take from 5% of one person's time up to requiring a full-time person. The executive-level sponsor with a vision and executive management support is critical to the success of e-business. In addition to requiring money, e-business done correctly will cause individuals' jobs to change and organizational structures to change. These changes can be difficult without proper executive support.

PURPOSE

It is important to understand and communicate the purpose of the e-business plan document and process. This essentially builds the case for action on why the company should invest in developing an e-business strategy and provides an introduction to the plan document. Document the purpose in the e-business plan document, but the section should be no more than one to two pages. It is a compelling, clear, and concise statement outlining the need for, or purpose of, an e-business plan. The following are the necessary components and questions to help develop the purpose section, as shown in Figure 3.2:

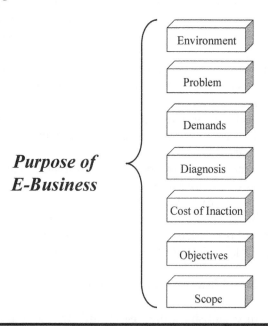

Figure 3.2   Purpose of E-Business

- **Environment:** What has happened or what has changed to cause concern about the current state of affairs? Have several e-business projects and initiatives been completed, but lacked an overall strategy, direction, and framework that encompass the initiatives and establish the roadmap for the future?
- **Problem:** What is the problem? Why is a plan or strategy necessary?
- **Demands:** What are the demands? What must be done? How was the effort initiated? How was the need perceived?
- **Diagnosis:** Why will the current methods not meet the demands?
- **Cost of Inaction:** What is the consequence of staying status quo? What will happen if an e-business strategy and plan are not developed? Will the company fall behind competition, and what would be the impact?
- **Objectives:** How will the organization know if the effort is successful? What are the guiding goals to developing an e-business plan? Is the purpose of the document to communicate the company's vision, direction, and objectives relative to e-business? Is the result of the process to understand the current e-business situation and identify e-business opportunities?
- **Scope:** What is the scope of the effort and the plan? Does it include all divisions, all geographic areas, and all parts of the business?

Figure 3.3 shows an example of a purpose section for an organization. ***Now draft the purpose section of your e-business plan document.***

IDENTIFY TEAM

Next, identify the team of individuals that will participate in the e-business initiative. Although some of the members will be consistent throughout the effort, additional business resources may be needed during the business planning phases (Phases 2 through 6), technical design resources in Phases 5 and 6, and technical resources during the implementation (Phases 6 and 7).

The following skills and attributes will be required of individuals on the e-business team:

- A good knowledge of the business
- Up-to-date knowledge of technology and how it can help the business
- Innovative, creative
- Industry knowledge
- Excellent communication skills
- Thorough

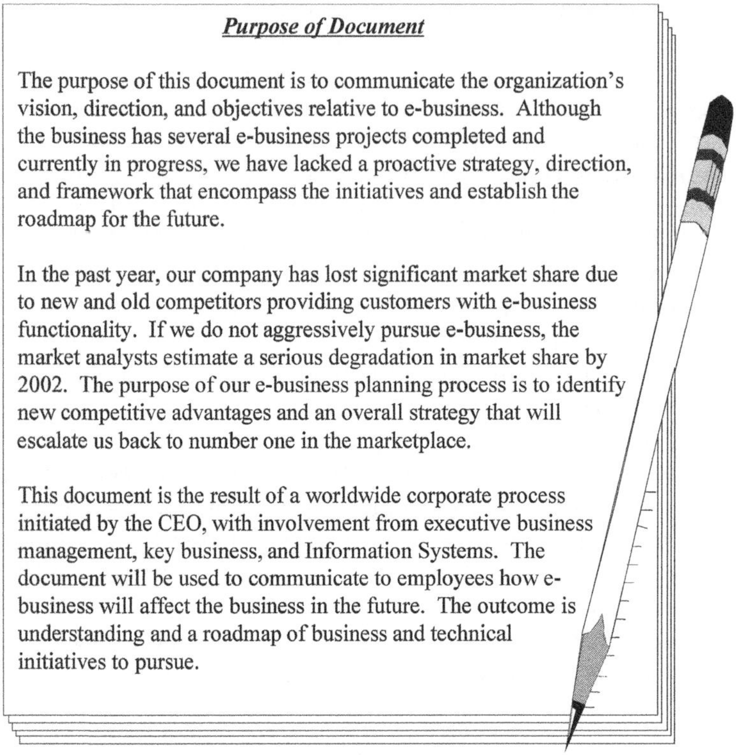

> ### *Purpose of Document*
>
> The purpose of this document is to communicate the organization's vision, direction, and objectives relative to e-business. Although the business has several e-business projects completed and currently in progress, we have lacked a proactive strategy, direction, and framework that encompass the initiatives and establish the roadmap for the future.
>
> In the past year, our company has lost significant market share due to new and old competitors providing customers with e-business functionality. If we do not aggressively pursue e-business, the market analysts estimate a serious degradation in market share by 2002. The purpose of our e-business planning process is to identify new competitive advantages and an overall strategy that will escalate us back to number one in the marketplace.
>
> This document is the result of a worldwide corporate process initiated by the CEO, with involvement from executive business management, key business, and Information Systems. The document will be used to communicate to employees how e-business will affect the business in the future. The outcome is understanding and a roadmap of business and technical initiatives to pursue.

Figure 3.3   Purpose

- Flexible
- Team player
- Ability and track record of delivering on time and within budget
- Well respected by the business and information systems group
- A methodology for planning and implementing e-business initiatives
- Experience in implementing e-business initiatives

After selecting the team of individuals, carefully select a project leader to lead the e-business initiative. In addition to the skills identified above, the e-business project leader should have all the following skills:

- Excellent project management skills and experience
- Passionate and a visionary about e-business and what it can do for the organization
- Organized
- Ability to coordinate many activities

- Ability to delegate
- Decisive
- Empowered

Consider whether the organization has the internal skills and resources that can be applied to implement e-business successfully. The organization may need to augment the internal skills with external assistance in some or all of the phases. In the new economy, it is not practical to try to do everything yourself, but rather to align with experts. Choose collaborative partners who take a true interest in the organization's success. When choosing a partner, consider the following points:

- Is the organization looking for one partner that is specialized in planning, and then a separate partner for the development and implementation? If engaging one partner to do both, make sure the partner does not slight the planning side and rush into implementation. Typically, firms either are strong in planning or in implementing rather than in both.
- Look for a partner who has a strong history and track record. The company should be well respected within its industry. Find out for how many companies the potential partner has planned or implemented a strategy. If considering an organization for implementation, look at the specific sites it has developed. How long has it been in business? Has the potential partner assisted companies in your specific industry? With what tools and technologies is the company experienced? Is the candidate a leader or follower in the e-business industry? How current is the candidate's experience?
- Review other plans the candidate has developed. Does the candidate have a solid and proven methodology that aligns with your organization's thoughts and principles?
- Obtain customer references and the total list of customers the candidate has assisted. Talk with previous customers to determine their levels of satisfaction. Talk with customers of the specific consultants who will be assigned to your project, not just customers of the firm. Have they completed other projects on time and within budget?
- Identify specific roles and responsibilities. What will be the expectations of individuals in the company as well as the external resources?
- Identify, meet, and review the credentials of the specific consultants who will be assigned to the project. Do they have the necessary experience and knowledge? Are you comfortable with them? Do you trust them?
- What is their approach to project management? How will the effort be planned and status and issues communicated?

- What is the cost? Is it fixed or variable? What are the variables?
- What is the timeline? What are the tasks that will be completed? What are the risks in the timeline?
- What is the return on investment?
- What is the process that will be utilized?
- How will success be measured?
- Who will have ownership of the deliverables?

PLANNING PROCESS

Now that you have management support, an executive sponsor, and a project team, the team can agree upon the process that will be used to develop the e-business plan. The planning process presented in this book can provide a general roadmap for the effort, but it may need to be tailored to meet the needs and environment of a particular organization and industry. Outline the process that will be utilized in your e-business plan document. This section can provide useful background to individuals reading the plan as to how the conclusions were reached. It also obtains agreement from the participants before the development of the plan as to the methodology the group agrees to use. Outline the initial process as well as how the plan will be kept up to date on an ongoing basis. Identify the governance process for ongoing e-business progress, including responsibilities, authority, and accountability. The following questions can help formulate the process section of the plan:

- What process will be utilized to develop the e-business plan?
- What are the underlying principles of the planning process?
- What phases are included in the process?
- What sections should be included in the table of contents of the plan document?
- How will the plan be kept up to date on an ongoing basis?
- How is the e-business planning process integrated with the company business planning process and information systems' planning process?
- Who is involved in the development of the e-business plan?
- What are the individual responsibilities of each member involved in the development? Is accountability clearly identified?
- Who is responsible for the ongoing maintenance of the e-business plan and what are their specific responsibilities?
- Who has decision-making authority for the e-business initiatives and direction?
- What is the process for obtaining funding for e-business initiatives?

Now draft the table of contents for your plan document as well as the planning process section of your e-business plan document.

COMMUNICATION PLAN

E-enabling a business can have a tremendous impact on the entire organization. E-business may impact individuals' jobs, responsibilities, organization, culture, and processes. It is critical to proactively create a communication and feedback vehicle to deliver information about the vision, strategy, plans, and progress of e-business projects. As with any major change, communication is critical, and lack of it can lead to failure. It is important to plan the internal communications vehicles to assist with the long-term success of the effort. Consider the following possibilities:

- Establish an e-business newsletter or include regular articles in an existing newsletter.
- Post the progress on an Intranet page.
- Provide regular e-mail updates and progress reports to all management.
- Provide regular updates at executive meetings.
- Provide presentations and updates at departmental meetings or all-employee meetings.

The objective is to fill the formal and informal communication channels with enough information to minimize the rumor mills filling in the blanks, which could negatively impact the progress of the project. Communication will also create support and excitement for the effort throughout the organization.

In addition to the communication plan to the organization, outline the internal communication plan for the project within the project team participants. It is critical to ensure that there is an open, honest, and constructive channel of communication throughout the entire team. Communication should be efficient so that bureaucracy does not slow the progress. Address the following:

- How will team members be kept informed of progress and decisions?
- How frequently will team meetings be held? What will be their purpose and who will participate?
- How will the executive sponsor be kept up to date?
- How will decisions be made?

ANNOUNCE

There is typically a lot of interest throughout the organization in e-business, and there might even be some unauthorized projects in progress in various places within the organization. Proactively announce the e-business initiative. Explain the following:

- Why is e-business important to the organization?
- What process will be utilized to develop an e-business strategy?
- What is the time frame on when a strategy will be defined?
- What is the time frame on when initial projects will be implemented?
- Who will be involved in the effort? Why were those individuals selected?
- How will others within the organization be impacted?

Your e-business initiative is now off to a great start. You have the management commitment, a passionate executive sponsor, a competent project team, and a communication plan. You have announced the effort to the organization. You are now ready to begin the work in defining the e-business strategy!

KEY POINTS TO REMEMBER

- Executive management support and a passionate executive business sponsor are critical to the success of an e-business initiative.
- Build a case for action in the purpose section of the e-business plan document.
- Identify a competent team of individuals and project leader for the e-business initiative.
- Consider whether internal resources need to be augmented with external assistance. Do not try to do everything yourself. Carefully select collaborative partners.
- Identify the planning process that will be used for the initial plan as well as ongoing updating.
- Proactively develop a communication and feedback vehicle to deliver information about the vision, strategy, plans, and progress of the e-business effort. A lack of communication can lead to failure.
- Proactively announce and promote the e-business effort throughout the organization.

NOTES FOR MY E-BUSINESS EFFORT

4

PHASE 2—DIAGNOSE

*"If in the last few years you hadn't discarded a major opinion
or acquired a new one, check your pulse. You may be dead."*

Gelett Burgess

As shown in Figure 4.1, the second phase of the e-business planning
process is **Diagnose**. In this phase, you will identify industry trends that
impact the company. It will also be necessary to document the company's
current e-business situation. The current situation will be analyzed. You
will diagnose the stakeholders and their process. You will also understand
the industry and external impact to the company. All players in the value
chain will be evaluated. The final step will be to evaluate the impact
e-business has on the business plan. At the end of this phase, you will
have completed the following sections in the e-business plan document:

- Trends
- Current Situation—Intranet, Internet, and Extranet
- Situation Analysis—Intranet, Internet, and Extranet
- Stakeholders
- Stakeholders' Process
- Industry Analysis
- Value Chain
- Business Analysis

Each of these sections is described in more detail below.

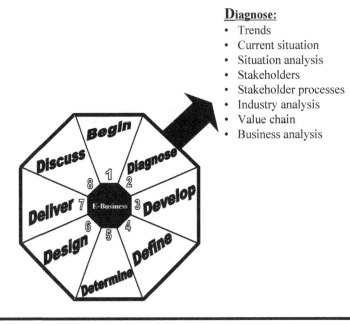

Diagnose:
- Trends
- Current situation
- Situation analysis
- Stakeholders
- Stakeholder processes
- Industry analysis
- Value chain
- Business analysis

Figure 4.1 Phase 2, Diagnose

TRENDS

Chapter 1 outlined many trends in business, applications, and technology. As part of your planning effort, it is now time to make sure that your management understands these industry trends and to discuss the impact these trends have on your business, customers, and industry. The following questions can help analyze how business trends impact your company:

- Has the organization experienced a shift from a cost reduction strategy to a business growth strategy? Should this shift have occurred? Does the company have the proper balance of cost reduction and business growth to be successful?
- Is there an increased speed at which business must occur? Is the company operating quickly enough?
- Has the company shifted from being self-contained to a global organization? If not, what additional changes are required to become a global organization?
- Has the company experienced increased collaboration within the industry? Who are the partners with whom the organization is collaborating? What is the networked web of value?
- Has the company changed from economies of scale to one-to-one relationships? How has this impacted the internal business processes?

■ Has the business focus shifted from internal to external? How?
■ Do customers have the ability for self-service? Does it need to be improved?
■ Is there an increased importance of processes? What are the critical processes?
■ What impact does the shift to virtual offices have on the company?
■ How have organizational structures changed to meet external requirements? How do they need to change to meet future requirements?
■ Has technology become a critical enabler to business rather than an afterthought?
■ What additional business trends impact the company?

The organization must also analyze how business application trends impact the organization. The following questions can help in this analysis:

■ Are improvements necessary in the areas of
    — Enterprise Requirements Planning (ERP)?
    — Customer Relationship Management (CRM)?
    — Supply Chain Management (SCM)?
    — Enterprise Application Integration (EAI)?
    — Changing Technical Infrastructure?
    — Knowledge Management (KM)?
    — Return on Investment (ROI) Applications?
    — Communication Applications?
■ What additional business application trends impact the company?

Next, review how technology trends impact the organization by asking the following questions:

■ What network improvements can be utilized in your company:
    — Increased connectivity?
    — Telecommunication advances?
    — Voice, data, video integration?
    — Increased use and reliance on the Internet?
■ What server improvements can be utilized at your company:
    — Decreased cost of a business transaction?
    — Increased interoperability and communication among diverse platforms?
    — Object-oriented programming?
    — Data synchronization ability?
    — Increased use of Java, HTML, XML, and other Web development and thin-client technologies?
    — Improved graphics, video, and sound?

     — Executive information systems?
     — Use of application service providers?
- What desktop and peripheral improvements can be utilized at your company:
     — Embedded, smaller, and more powerful processors and chips?
     — Wireless, cellular, and mobile technology?
     — Easy-to-use interfaces?
     — Voice recognition?
     — Multi-modal access, hand-held and PDA devices?
     — Computer telephone integration?
     — Pen-based computers and other mobile devices?
     — Bar coding?
     — Smart cards?
     — Encryption, biometrics, and other security measures?
- What additional technology trends impact the company?

Finally, prioritize the trends based on their impact to the company, timing, and likelihood of occurrence.

Now draft the trends section of your e-business plan document.

CURRENT SITUATION

It is important to have a thorough understanding of the company's current e-business environment before entertaining improvements. Just about every company has some Internet presence and functionality in place. The following questions will help develop the current situation section:

- What functionality does the company's Intranet currently have? Outline the general areas of information and purpose. How much is the Intranet used?
- What is the technical environment that supports the Intranet? Identify the hardware server, operating system, and version.
- What people support the Intranet environment? What do they do? What are their individual responsibilities?
- What processes support the Intranet environment, directly and indirectly? How are changes made? How are changes prioritized? How are changes tested?

Answer the same questions for the Internet and Extranet environments. It is important that the current situation section contain only the facts, with no personal opinions or judgments. It also needs to outline what is there today, not what is planned for the future.

Now draft the current situation section of the e-business plan document for the Intranet, Internet, and Extranet environments.

SITUATION ANALYSIS

You are now ready to analyze the current situation. The strategy has not been developed yet, so you are not looking at the gap, but rather analyzing what is good and what could be improved regarding the current situation based on what is known today. List the strengths and areas of improvement of the overall e-business environment as well as each of the environments including the Intranet, Internet, and Extranet. A thorough and objective analysis of the current situation can immediately identify areas to improve and strengthen. As you go through the remainder of the planning steps, you can confirm and strengthen the opportunities for improvement and build on the areas of strength.

Figures 4.2, 4.3, 4.4, and 4.5 show examples of a situation analysis of overall environment, Intranet, Internet, and Extranet environments, respectively.

It is also extremely helpful to attempt to quantify the current situation. This can be useful when benchmarking or comparing future progress. Do not spend a tremendous amount of effort getting total agreement on the exact scores, but rather obtain a general consensus on the state of affairs.

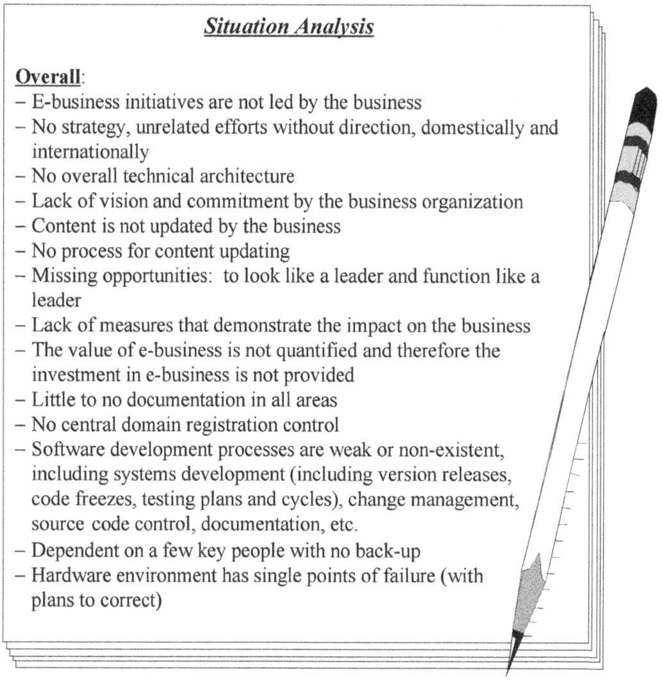

Situation Analysis

Overall:
- E-business initiatives are not led by the business
- No strategy, unrelated efforts without direction, domestically and internationally
- No overall technical architecture
- Lack of vision and commitment by the business organization
- Content is not updated by the business
- No process for content updating
- Missing opportunities: to look like a leader and function like a leader
- Lack of measures that demonstrate the impact on the business
- The value of e-business is not quantified and therefore the investment in e-business is not provided
- Little to no documentation in all areas
- No central domain registration control
- Software development processes are weak or non-existent, including systems development (including version releases, code freezes, testing plans and cycles), change management, source code control, documentation, etc.
- Dependent on a few key people with no back-up
- Hardware environment has single points of failure (with plans to correct)

Figure 4.2   Overall Situation Analysis

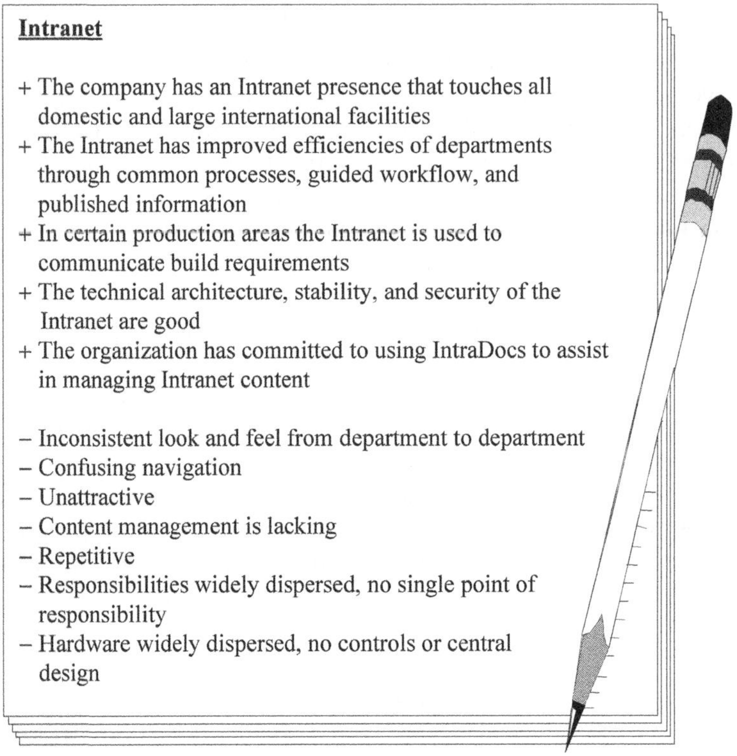

Intranet

+ The company has an Intranet presence that touches all domestic and large international facilities
+ The Intranet has improved efficiencies of departments through common processes, guided workflow, and published information
+ In certain production areas the Intranet is used to communicate build requirements
+ The technical architecture, stability, and security of the Intranet are good
+ The organization has committed to using IntraDocs to assist in managing Intranet content

− Inconsistent look and feel from department to department
− Confusing navigation
− Unattractive
− Content management is lacking
− Repetitive
− Responsibilities widely dispersed, no single point of responsibility
− Hardware widely dispersed, no controls or central design

Figure 4.3   Intranet Situation Analysis

This scorecard can also help identify strengths or weaknesses. Exhibit 4.1 is an example of an e-business scorecard that could be utilized.

Now draft the situation analysis section of the e-business plan document, including the Intranet, Internet, and Extranet environments. Also complete the e-business scorecard.

STAKEHOLDERS

A stakeholder is any external entity that has an interest in the success or operation of the company. The customer is the obvious and most important stakeholder in today's environment. Every company has customers: businesses have whoever uses the product or service, government has the citizens, nonprofits have the people whose needs they serve. Consider not only the direct customers (such as distributors, agents, brokers, retailers, and dealers), but also the end customer or consumer. Just because the company may rely on a strong distribution or intermediary network today, do not

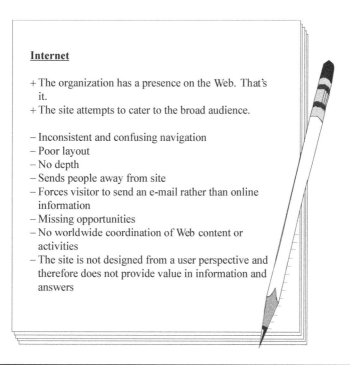

Internet

+ The organization has a presence on the Web. That's it.
+ The site attempts to cater to the broad audience.

− Inconsistent and confusing navigation
− Poor layout
− No depth
− Sends people away from site
− Forces visitor to send an e-mail rather than online information
− Missing opportunities
− No worldwide coordination of Web content or activities
− The site is not designed from a user perspective and therefore does not provide value in information and answers

Figure 4.4   Internet Situation Analysis

ignore the end customers and their desires. As an example, a hearing aid manufacturer may have the following stakeholders:

- Patients
- Patients' families
- Professionals
   — Audiologists
   — Dispensers
   — Clinics
   — Hospitals
- Public
- Government
- Partners or suppliers
- Employees

As another example, Microsoft identified its customers as:*

- Information technology managers
- Knowledge workers

* Siegel, David, *Futurize Your Enterprise*, John Wiley & Sons, New York, p. 5.

Extranet

+The company has an Extranet that is a formal offering to its customers
+ The services offered link to back end systems and provide value
+ Order Status, Order History, Financial Status

− Brochureware exists but is not used
− There are no drivers for business units to encourage customers to use the Extranet
− Key functionality is weak and not supported by the organization
− Order desk is weak…no vision, strategy, or commitment to improve business processes through the order desk
− Content is shallow
− Dead links exist
− Some functionality lacks a purpose
− Confusing organization, inconsistent and confusing navigation
− Poor layout
− Missing opportunities
− The company has not demonstrated aggressive desire to implement applications
− Lack of systems development processes
− Programming languages and tools are outdated
− Vendor-dependent application architecture
− Single points of hardware failure
− Single point of knowledge; one developer, administrator

Figure 4.5 Extranet Situation Analysis

■ Software developers
■ Consumers

A study by Meta Group interviewed 800 business and Information Technology executives and found that most companies (83%) lacked the data to build a comprehensive view of their customers, as Figure 4.6 shows.* Four out of five of the companies surveyed said that they do not have a complete view of their customers, even though 92% said that improved customer intimacy is an important priority. Also, 70% of those companies collecting data do not believe they are effectively using the information that they gathered. Many companies are struggling with systems and processes to collect and integrate customer data. In the Meta study,

---

* "Companies in the Dark about Customers," *InformationWeek*, May 1, 2000, p. 177, www.informationweek.com.

Exhibit 4.1   E-Business Scorecard

Ranking:

1:   No systematic approach is evident to the criteria; results do not exist or are poor

2:   Beginning of a systematic approach is evident but major gaps exist

3:   A systematic approach to the criteria with good performance

4:   A sound and systematic approach to the criteria with good to excellent performance

5:   Criteria are fully implemented without any significant weaknesses or gaps in any area

Criteria	Intranet Ranking	Internet Ranking	Extranet Ranking
Strategy:			
■ A comprehensive e-business strategy exists with all opportunities identified and prioritized			
■ The e-business strategy is aligned and integrated with the business strategy			
■ E-business competitive comparisons have been completed			
■ The vision for e-business is known and communicated (marketed) throughout the organization			
■ There is an e-business mindset within the organization, open to and aggressively pursuing the opportunities			
■ The e-business strategy is seamless and consistent across all parts of the organization			
■ Back-office systems have a clear direction on how to support e-business and are moving in that direction			
■ Business areas, not Information Systems, drive the e-business efforts			
■ There is process for continually planning and adjusting the e-business strategy			
■ All employees understand the e-business strategy			
■ There is proper funding to meet the e-business initiatives			
■ The business is perceived as a leader in the industry and functionality is provided to obtain a competitive advantage			

Exhibit 4.1   E-Business Scorecard (continued)

People:			
■ Responsibilities are identified and documented and individuals are held accountable for performance			
■ There is appropriate back-up of responsibilities and knowledge for e-business areas			
■ There is a strong business sponsor with a passion for e-business			
■ The appropriate business units are responsible for content			
■ Cross-functional teams exist to improve processes			
■ Metrics exist for assessing specific impacts of e-business on the organization			
■ Proper orientation and training is provided for e-business resources			
■ Incentives are provided to encourage the business to develop and promote e-solutions			
■ Change management is proactively considered in implementing e-business			
■ E-business projects are delivered on time, on budget with proper functionality			
■ Key customers are tied into the e-business environment and strategy			
■ Key suppliers and business partners are tied into the e-business environment and strategy			
■ The organization learns and implements improvements to new business initiatives			
■ The skill set of the e-business team is adequate to do the job			
■ Sufficient resources are assigned to reach the e-business goals			
Processes:			
■ There is a systems development process that manages application life cycle, including version releases, code freezes, testing plans and cycles, change			

Exhibit 4.1   E-Business Scorecard (continued)

management, source code control, and documentation			
■ Changes are grouped in a release mode and the change management process is managed			
■ There is a test plan that is used for testing			
■ Stress tests are completed when necessary			
■ Changes are documented			
■ There is a process defined for updating content			
■ There is a process and escalation procedure for unhappy customers			
■ Domain registration is controlled and managed centrally			
■ There is a usage policy			
■ Business processes have been engineered to support the use of each application			
■ Service level agreements are in place and met			
■ Metrics are utilized to measure and report the value of e-business initiatives			
■ Individuals review metrics and reports on a regular basis and take appropriate action as necessary			
■ Updated documentation exists for the functionality and systems			
Business Functionality:			
■ Functionality is designed from the customer viewpoint			
■ Content is provided for all the stakeholders			
■ Business applications are fully integrated as necessary			
■ Functionality addresses all worldwide facilities consistently			
■ All key information is available online			
■ Navigation is consistent and easy to follow			
■ Content supports the business direction and function at an appropriate depth			

Exhibit 4.1 E-Business Scorecard (continued)

■ Customer input is received on a regular basis and acted upon within 1 day; content is updated as necessary by the business			
■ Attractive and consistent look and feel that fits the environment			
■ Customers can quickly find answers to their most frequently asked questions			
■ Customers can easily check the status of their orders or requests			
■ Customers consistently return to the site			
■ Automated e-mails are utilized to develop a customer relationship			
Technical Infrastructure: ■ Single points of failure and redundancy are addressed			
■ Disaster recovery plans and back-up processes are in place			
■ Documentation exists for the technical architecture			
■ There is a planned, consistent, and up-to-date architecture			
■ Key metrics are captured and reported on a regular basis			
■ Proper security and firewalls are in place			
■ Infrastructure is scalable			
■ Information is restricted to those who need access			
■ There is sufficient capacity			
■ A network management tool is utilized			
■ Proper standards exist, including Web browser, Web development application software, hardware and other software			
■ Antivirus measures are in place			

56% of the companies indicated that improving customer intimacy was one of the top three business priorities while an additional 36% said it ranked among the top 10 business priorities.

This step of the e-business strategy development is critical. If this step is missed, the target will be missed on the e-business strategy. Determine who the stakeholders are and what they want. Although it may seem like

Does your company know who its customer are?

Yes
17%

No
83%

Figure 4.6 Customer Knowledge

an easy or obvious question, it may be a surprising revelation as all the detailed questions are answered. The following questions will assist in identifying the stakeholders:

- Who are all the stakeholders, including customers, suppliers, public, employees, partners, and government?
- Who are the direct customers?
- Who are the indirect customers? Who are the end customers?
- What are the categories of customers and the amount of sales and transactions?
- Who are the potential customers?
- Who are the customers desired in the future?
- What are the most profitable customer segments today and in the future?
- How static is the customer base?
- What are the demographics of the current customer base?
- What is the purchase and interaction history of current customers?
- Which groups have the most influence on customer purchasing decisions?
- What customers generate referrals?
- What is the customer retention rate?
- What is the customer retention rate for targeted customers?
- What are customer service costs by customer segment?
- Does the company have a single accurate database of all the customer information that is necessary? If not, how can it be developed?
- Who are the suppliers?
- What are the categories of suppliers and the amount of business transactions and cost?

- Who in the public would be interested in the company? Why?
- Who are the key partners? How beneficial or critical are these partners?
- Who are the key partners desired in the future?
- What government agencies have an impact on the company?

Next, understand more about the customers and what they want from the business. For example:

- To be able to get all the information that is needed from the Web site with powerful search abilities
- The ability to communicate in native language and currency
- To be able to obtain information or service 24 hours a day, 7 days a week anywhere in the world
- To receive quick, personalized information, service, and experience that doesn't waste time
- To be able to easily understand the information
- To be able to find out whom to call if it is desired to speak to someone
- To receive immediate (or at least within the same day) response to e-mails
- To be able to find answers to questions and help themselves
- To interact seamlessly by telephone, palm, Internet, e-mail, voice response, or mail
- To be able to get one-stop shopping, even with several accounts with other locations or divisions
- A broad selection of quality goods and services
- To be able to place an order on the Web site
- To be able to customize the product or service to individual needs
- To obtain fair value for the price
- To get accurate price and delivery information
- To receive immediate electronic confirmations on orders or requests
- To easily find or know the status of an order online
- To obtain an order quickly
- To obtain invoices electronically
- To pay invoices electronically
- Complete product or service guarantees with easy, hassle-free returns
- Anyone the customer interacts with to be knowledgeable of any previous transactions or conversations the customer has had with the company no matter what office or person the customer has worked with in the past
- All information and personal profile on file after providing it only once
- To feel that each person is important and valued, and that the individual's business matters
- To be assured that information is secure

- Accurate service and response to requests
- To obtain trouble-shooting, service, replacement parts, and replacement instructions online
- Proactive service
- To be asked for individual opinions on how to improve the product and service

Companies that can satisfy all these requirements are easy to do business with. Try doing business with your company and see how many of these requirements the company can fulfill. It might be surprising how many improvements may be necessary! Although the list of requirements for companies may seem long, some companies, particularly leaders in their industry, are able to meet all of the requirements. Customer requirements typically increase with time. The list of requirements today may seem minor compared to what customers will require 3 years from now. Think about the interactions when you are a customer. Many companies have made improvements that actually raised the bar of expectations for a particular industry and forced their competitors to match or beat their functionality and technology to meet customer demands such as:

- Rental cars with easy return of the car by agents with hand-held devices
- Airlines with electronic check-in and tickets
- Banking, allowing electronic payment of bills and automatic deposit
- Automobile automatic emergency assistance
- Shipping companies that allow tracking the status of a package

Does the organization want to lead the industry by providing what the customers want, or be forced to do so by the competition? What do customers want from the company? The following detailed questions can help answer that question:

- What are the interests of customers?
- Why do customers come to the organization?
- Are customers happy with the business? Why or why not?
- Who else have customers considered for their needs? Why?
- How can the Internet help the business to give customers what they want?
- What do potential customers want?
- What are the preferences as to how customers want to be treated?
- What makes customers successful today? What will make them successful in the future?
- Is the business getting true customer input to really know what customers want?

- How can new customers be acquired?
- How can customers be retained?
- How can existing customer accounts be grown?
- What would customers change about the relationship with the company if they could?
- What new advances could benefit customers that they may not realize are possible?

In order for the business to be successful, it is critical to understand the end customers and what they value. Establish processes to regularly obtain input and comments from customers. Customer focus groups, user groups, customer interviews, incentives to encourage online comments, and regular interactions with customers should all be part of the regular business processes. It can be harmful to be insulated from direct customer feedback by always working with the middle organization, such as distributors or dealers. It may take extra effort to forge a relationship with the end customer, but it is always well worth the effort. For example, software purchased through local electronic stores usually contains warranty registration cards or information to collect end-customer information. Once the company has that valuable information, it never asks the customer for it again, other than to verify it. It may seem like obtaining customer information on small commodity items would be impossible, but it is not. Hallmark (www.hallmark. com) is a great example. Although Hallmark sells a large number of cards to millions of customers, it has begun the process to become customer intimate. Hallmark has a Web site with many useful tools that can be used once a profile is entered. A customer can establish reminders for important dates (birthdays, anniversaries), and Hallmark will send an e-mail reminder to the customer specified a number of days before the important date. Hallmark has started to create a valuable database of its customers and its customers' important dates that require its product! Hallmark can launch many other services using this valuable database of information.

The key to business success is to determine who the customers are and what they want, and to forge strong relationships with them. Build community, build a useful customer database, provide self service, and provide personalized service.

Now draft the stakeholder's section of your e-business plan document.

STAKEHOLDERS' PROCESSES

After understanding who the stakeholders are and what they want from the business, it is important to understand the process used by the stakeholder. One approach to understanding customers is understanding how they engage or want to engage with the company. In other words,

Customer Process

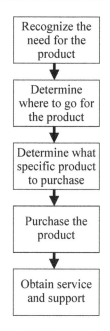

Figure 4.7   Customer Process

what steps does the stakeholder take to know about the company, engage the company, and establish a relationship with the company? For example, a customer might have the process outlined in Figure 4.7 and a supplier might have the process outlined in Figure 4.8.

A typical process for a customer may include:

- **Awareness:** How does the prospective customer become aware of and introduced to the company and product?
- **Evaluation:** How does the prospective customer evaluate the options and consider the company or product unique from others?
- **Engage:** How does the prospective customer become a customer and engage in business with the company?
- **Support:** How does the customer receive follow-up service, support, and sales?
- **Community:** How does the customer provide referrals and sell others?

The following questions will help understand the stakeholders' processes:

- What steps or processes do customers (indirect or end customers) go through to select and buy the product or service?
- What steps or processes do the direct customers go through to select and buy the product or service?

Supplier Process

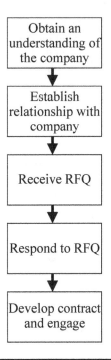

Figure 4.8   Supplier Process

- How does the company interact with customers?
- How can the customer process be streamlined?
- What steps or processes do suppliers go through to have a relationship with the company?
- How can the suppliers' processes be streamlined?
- Does the business have control over the customer's entire process?
- What topics of information is the public interested in?
- What topics of information do employees need?
- How often do the stakeholders (including customers, suppliers, others) use the Internet? How technology literate or averse are the stakeholders?
- What are the various points of interaction that the company may have with the customer and various stakeholders?
- How can the company engage customers in the order, production, and delivery process?

Now draft the stakeholder's section of your e-business plan document.

INDUSTRY ANALYSIS

In addition to a thorough understanding of the stakeholders, it is also important to have a thorough understanding of your industry, what is happening and changing in the industry and its distribution channels. Industry changes may significantly impact your business strategy as well as your e-business strategy. Companies not aware of industry changes could find their business models out of date and their businesses extinct.

The Internet can be a terrific source of information on the industry. Internet sources for industry information as shown in Figure 4.9 include:

■ Competitors' Web sites
■ Industry journals may have articles referencing activities of competitors
  — www.individual.com provides industry-specific news clippings
  — www.cahners.com has a variety of industry-specific trade publications
■ Technology journals may have articles referencing activities of competitors
  — *Information Week* (www.informationweek.com)
  — *CIO* (www.cio.com)
  — *Computerworld* (www.computerworld.com)
  — *InfoWorld* (www.infoworld.com)
  — *CRM* (www.crmmag.com)
  — *eAI Journal* (www.eaijournal.com)
  — *eWeek* (www.eweek.com)
  — *Internetweek* (www.internetweek.com)

Competitor Information

Web site

Software products

Industry journals

Industry associations

Technology journals

Industry portals

Research companies

Figure 4.9   Competitor Information

- Research companies (typically involve a charge):
  - Giga (www.gigaweb.com)
  - Gartner Group (www.gartner.com)
  - Meta (www.metagroup.com)
- Industry portals and searches:
  - www.business.com and www.office.com have general information on industries
  - www.hoovers.com lists industries or companies
  - www.vertical.net provides vertical portals for a wide variety of industries
  - www.dowjones.wsj.com provides industry-specific resources
  - www.corporateinformation.com provides links to industry data and company profiles, information by company, industry, or country
  - www.edgar-online.com posts the latest filings, quarterly and annual reports, ownership statements, insider trades, and mergers and acquisitions
  - www.company.sleuth.com compiles news, insider trades, and registrations of Internet domains, trademarks, and patents
  - www.yahoo.com can search on industry or words that describe the industry
- Industry associations can provide competitor information:
  - www.vcanet.org has a directory of associations
  - www.asaenet.org/find also has a directory of associations
  - www.tscentral.com is a directory of trade shows
- Software products:
  - www.alexa.com provides free software to analyze Web sites and provide information
  - Liaison Express tracks product and pricing information from Web sites of competitors and suppliers, enabling immediate responses to price cuts and promotions
  - Caesius Software Inc. has a product called WebQL (www.webql.com) that can be used to gather information about competitors
  - www.rivalwatch.com can also provide competitor information

Employees (or even individuals interviewing for positions) who come from competitor companies can also be sources of information. Interview individuals within the company who have a good knowledge of the industry. Industry presentations, trade shows, and associations may feature company activities or have employees in attendance who would provide information. Talk to customers and suppliers. Internal processes should be established so any employee who has information about a competitor can easily share it via an Intranet.

The following questions help understand the industry:

- Who are the competitors?
- What are each competitor's strengths and weaknesses?
- Are there a lot of competitors, or a few large competitors? What companies dominate the industry? How might this change in the future?
- What might competition look like in the future due to market expansion, product expansion, backward integration, forward integration, change in fortune, or e-business?
- What is the total industry size today? In the future?
- What are the distribution channels?
- What changes or technologies would revolutionize the industry if they were implemented?
- What are future technologies that will impact the industry?
- What are the largest e-business threats to the business?
- How can the Internet change the business?
- What impact will e-business have on the retail channel and the distribution channel?
- What impact will e-business have on the price structure?
- What impact will e-business have on existing business?
- What channel expansion or disintermediation is possible?
- What types of distribution channel conflict may arise?
- What is the company's channel strategy?
- What companies are allies?
- How can the company reach new customers and new markets?
- What is the impact on marketing and branding strategies?
- Are there any governmental or regulatory changes impacting the industry?
- What are barriers to entry in the market? For example, high capital costs, high customer switching costs, strong customer loyalty, regulation, and patents.
- What are barriers to exit in the market? For example, expensive equipment that is difficult to sell, long-term labor contracts, extended customer leases and commitments, service agreements, and government regulations.
- What other alternatives do customers have for the product?
- Do market assumptions need to be redefined?

Now draft the industry analysis section of your e-business plan document.

VALUE CHAIN

In addition to the industry, an in-depth understanding and redesign of the value chain is important. The value chain is a combination of business processes that create value by delivering goods or services to the customer. Every company, whether it delivers a product or a service, has a value chain. An organization's internal value chain includes product planning, procurement, manufacturing, order fulfillment, service, and support. However, the complete value chain extends back to include all the organizations that produce raw materials or other functions that enable the organization to deliver the end value, or solution, to the customer, as shown in Figure 4.10. Although many people refer to the value chain as the supply chain, the value chain is more descriptive of the new economy with complex webs of value rather than linear supply chains. Companies that do not provide a distinct value in the process will quickly be eliminated from the traditional supply chain.

An integrated value chain can deliver the products or services more efficiently and effectively to the customer, thereby creating greater value. Organizations within an integrated value chain view one other as collaborative partners, or an extended enterprise, and share information to achieve agility, speed, and reduced costs. As Chapter 1 identified, the industry is moving from linear and sequential supply chains to networked webs of value providing units. If any company in the value chain aggressively pursues e-business while the other participants lag in e-business, the company can drastically change and challenge the entire value chain. Therefore, redesigning and reviewing the value chain is not an option, but a requirement for survival.

Some companies may fear or feel limited with e-business because they have built a substantial dealer or distributor network that they do not want

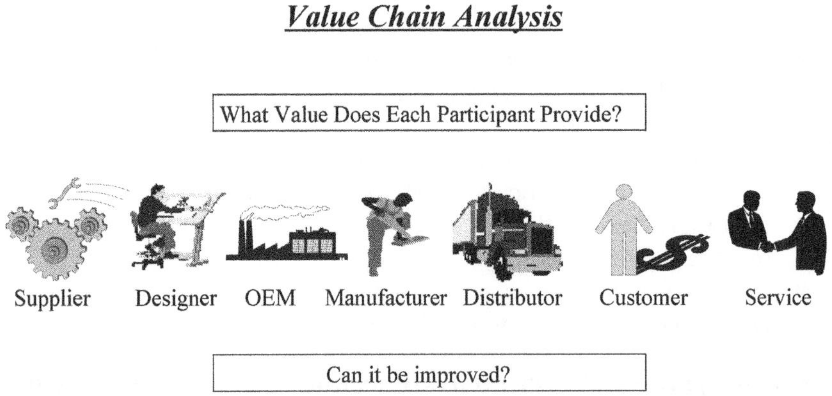

Value Chain Analysis

Figure 4.10   Value Chain Analysis

to disturb or upset. However, this should not hinder a company's plans, as there are many ways to complement or work with an existing channel. Many companies have successfully implemented e-business without disturbing an existing distributor channel. E-business can help support dealers and distributors rather than threaten their existence. Many times, action must be taken to meet customer requirements and remain competitive. A friend visited a boat manufacturer while on vacation in Florida. Because she was in the market to purchase a new boat, she thought it would be beneficial to see the manufacturing process and inquire about purchasing the boat directly, thus eliminating the additional costs of going through a distributor. During the tour, she raised the question of purchasing a boat over the Internet. As there were distributors on the tour, the tour guide was defensive and the distributors quickly explained the value they add to the process. As a customer, she felt that customer preferences were ignored, because she just wanted a boat without the additional services provided by the distributors. Cars and other vehicles can be purchased over the Internet, why not their boat? The boat could be ordered over the Internet and picked up at the nearest distributor. Companies must learn how to manage their old distribution strategies while still taking advantage of the power of the Internet.

The following questions help understand the value chain that the company participates in:

- What are the steps in the value chain?
- Where are the weak links in the value chain?
- What is the role of the business in the value chain?
- Can the company work with others to add more value more efficiently?
- Do others have assets the company can utilize?
- What impact will increased connectivity have on the value of your brand?
- How can the entire value stream be re-engineered?
- How can steps be simplified? Can steps be combined?
- Can the order of steps be changed?
- Can the process be accelerated? Can the timing change?
- Have parallel industries cut major steps from the process? How?

Now draft the value chain section of your e-business plan document.

BUSINESS ANALYSIS

It is important to have an honest self-portrait of the business situation as it exists today. The best way to do this is through development of the traditional **s**trengths, **w**eaknesses, **o**pportunities, and **t**hreats (or SWOT) analysis. This analysis of strengths will provide information to help identify how the business can maintain and extend the competitive advantages it has today by identifying areas to capitalize on. Weaknesses, or areas of improvement, will identify areas to improve, monitor, or eliminate as well as identify areas that may impact the ability to execute a strategic direction.

The following questions assist in the development of the SWOT analysis:

Strengths:

- What are the internal strengths of the business? Are there any new strengths relative to e-business and Internet capabilities?
- What is the business good at doing?
- What capabilities, resources, and skills can the business draw upon to carry out the strategies?
- Why do customers buy from the company?
- What is the company's competitive advantage?
- Why do employees stay at the company?
- Consider and rate the critical areas, such as management, organization, customer base, research and development, operations, sales and marketing, distribution and delivery, and financial condition.

Weaknesses, or areas of improvement:

- What are the internal weaknesses of the business?
- What is the business not good at doing?
- What deficiencies may hinder the business from achieving the strategies?
- Why might the company lose a sale or customer?
- Why do employees quit the company?

Opportunities:

- What are possible shifts in technology with e-business and Internet?
- How might availability of new materials change with e-business?
- What are new customer categories with the Internet-enabled world?
- Why might there be sudden spurts or changes in market growth?
- Are there any new uses for old product?
- Can the business get access to highly skilled people through the use of Internet technology?
- Can the business reach new locations and geographies with the Internet?
- Would any new organization models be useful?
- Are there any new distribution channels available as a result of the Internet?
- Are there any potential changes to laws or regulations?

Threats:

- Might there be market slowdowns?
- Is there any legislation that might be costly?
- Are there any changing trends due to technology?

- Is there new and aggressive competition resulting from the Internet?
- Are there substitute products?
- Is there exchange-rate volatility?
- Might there be a shortage of any raw material?
- Are there any potential changes in patent protections?
- Are there any potential changes in labor agreements?
- Has the product saturated the market?

Now draft the business analysis section of your e-business plan document.

Congratulations! You have successfully diagnosed the current situation, both internally and externally. You can now go on to develop how the company will function in the new economy.

KEY POINTS TO REMEMBER

- Identify how business trends, business application trends, and technology trends impact the business, customers, and industry.
- Thoroughly document the current situation, including the Intranet, Internet, and Extranet environments.
- Analyze the current situation utilizing an e-business scorecard.
- Carefully identify all the stakeholders, including customers and their desires.
- Identify the stakeholders' processes.
- Analyze the industry.
- Redesign the value chain and clarify the role of the business in the new value chain economy.

NOTES FOR MY E-BUSINESS EFFORT

_____

_____

_____

_____

_____

_____

_____

_____

_____

_____

_____

_____

_____

_____

_____

_____

_____

_____

_____

_____

_____

_____

_____

5

PHASE 3—DEVELOP

"I do not believe you can do today's job with yesterday's methods and be in business tomorrow."

Nelson Jackson

The third phase of the e-business planing process is **Develop**. As Figure 5.1 shows, in this phase you will develop the value proposition, business plan impact, overall strategy, and metrics to measure progress. At the end of this phase, you will have completed the following sections in the e-business plan document:

- Value Proposition
- Value Delivery Proposition
- Strategy
- Metrics

VALUE PROPOSITION

Success in the networked economy is dependent upon a company concisely establishing its value propositions, or core competencies. No longer can companies afford to fund activities outside of their core competencies. In the fluid, networked economy facilitated by the Internet and e-business, companies must select what they do the best and outsource or forgo the rest.

In the past, value propositions were often inward looking, focusing on the product or processes. With the customer as the center in the new economy, value propositions must have an outward focus. A value proposition is what the business is trying to achieve for the customer. Or, from the customer vantage point, the value the customer wants from

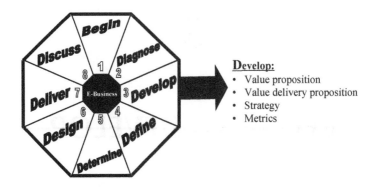

Develop:
- Value proposition
- Value delivery proposition
- Strategy
- Metrics

Figure 5.1   Phase 3, Develop

the business. The value proposition must be continually reviewed because competition is trying to make the value obsolete.

Some questions to ask when developing the value proposition include:

- What does the customer value? Does the customer value cross-selling, up-selling, new or updated products and services, supply chain efficiencies, decreased cycle times, or faster time-to-market? Go back to the list of items in Chapter 4 that were identified as potential desires of a customer. Which of these are important to your customers?
- What does the customer not value and is not willing to pay for?
- What does the customer not value today but will in the future?
- What value would delight customers and exceed their expectations?
- How will e-business change the customer expectations?
- How can a new value proposition be created for the customer?
- What new forms of value can be created?
- How can the business build loyalty and maintain customers in the connected economy? How can the customer be encouraged to do business with the business and not with competitors?
- What do customers have in common? How could they gain value from one another in a community?

The following is a value proposition from one company:

- Provide knowledge and promote learning
- Focus on the preferences and needs of individuals
- Simplify the ease of doing business
- Provide complete customer solutions

Now draft the value proposition section of your e-business plan document.

VALUE DELIVERY PROPOSITION

Now that it is understood what the customers value, how is the business going to provide that value? The value delivery proposition is how the product or service will get the business closer to the goal, or the stated values. Some questions to ask when developing the value delivery proposition include:

- How is the business positioned to deliver the value?
- How is the competition positioned to deliver the value?
- Can other entities provide the same value?
- How can the business model change to better deliver the value?
- Can the business expand value by moving up or down the distribution channel?
- Can the business transform from a commodity offering to a total experience offering?
- Can the business change the delivery of the value?
- What challenges or barriers will the company face?
- How can the business be designed to meet customer expectations?
- How can the customer experience be improved?
- Can the business create a totally new experience for the customer?
- How can the business make the product/service faster?
- How can the business make the product/service more convenient?
- How can the business make the product/service more personalized or customized? How can the business deliver personalized service?
- How can the business offer the product/service at a lower price?
- How can the business offer the product/service at higher quality?
- How can the business own the customer's total experience? How much control does the business have over the total customer experience (including learning about productions, selecting, quoting, purchasing, delivery, setup, installation, after-care, service, purchasing follow-on products, taking delivery, invoicing, resolving disputes).
- Does the business provide a 360-degree view of the customer relationship (i.e., whoever takes the call has access to records of the customer relationship even if it is with another department?) Can the customer access information about all his/her accounts or issues?
- Can customers help themselves?
- How can the business utilize technology to do things it is not currently doing?
- How can the business increase flexibility and responsiveness?
- How can the business be more efficient and effective?

Review the work developed in the second phase of the e-business planning process to help identify how the business can create new value delivery, including:

- The customer process: How can the customer process be streamlined?
- The business strengths, weaknesses, opportunities, and threats: How can the business take advantage of the strengths and minimize the weaknesses? How can the business aggressively take advantage of the opportunities and diminish the threats?
- The industry analysis: How can the business impact the competitors and industry?
- The value chain: How can the business re-engineer the value chain?

The value delivery proposition has the potential to totally change the industry, or even create a new industry. Some examples of companies that changed the value delivery proposition include:

- Free e-mail services or music sites that changed from a subscription or purchase model to an advertising model
- Grocery distributors that offer online services directly to the consumer rather than just to grocery stores, thus moving down the supply chain
- Consulting companies that sell information or provide online consulting or seminars rather than requiring on-site consultants for expertise
- Bidding and auction sites that changed the concept of fixed prices
- Marketing lead management firms that provide leads to the sales person's palm pilot, thus changing the delivery function
- Smart measurement devices that automatically call the company for preventive maintenance or replacement parts, thus locking in the supplier/customer relationship

Now draft the value delivery proposition section of your e-business plan document.

STRATEGY

Next is the important task of developing the e-business strategy. As part of the strategy development, go back to the business plan and analyze the impact and possibly update the business plan. The business plan and the e-business strategy must complement each other and work together.

To summarize what you have done so far, you have identified the stakeholders and customers and identified their processes. You have analyzed the industry, value chain, and your business. You have identified what value you are going to provide your customer and how you are going to deliver that value. Next, you will summarize this into a strategy.

The difference between this e-business methodology and traditional business planning models is that we started with the customer as the center of the universe and worked out. Traditional business planning models will start here with the strategy, defining what the company wants to be.

Look at the value proposition and value delivery proposition that was just formulated and summarize the e-business strategy. The following questions will help develop the strategy:

- How will the business create value in the future? Is it to reach more and new types of customers, providing cross-selling and up-selling? Is it through new or updated products or services, new packaging and pricing approaches? Is it through supply, service, or distribution chain efficiencies? Is it through decreased cycle times, faster time-to-market?
- How can the business use e-business to meet customer needs as well as the business goals and objectives?
- Is the business a market leader or follower with e-business? Where does the business want to be?
- Will the business take an aggressive e-business approach to e-enabling the entire enterprise and processes, or will it utilize e-business in a targeted approach to provide information, enhance service, facilitate transactions, or provide targeted communities?
- What are the driving objectives the business will utilize e-business to accomplish? For example, is the business going to use e-business to reduce costs, generate leads, increase revenue, improve communication, develop brands, enable new business models, launch a new product, or train employees?
- What new opportunities does the Internet provide?
- What additional markets can the company reach?
- What does the business do well to satisfy customers and how can it be ported and exploited in the electronic playing field of the Internet?
- What role can the Internet play in helping the company meet the value proposition and value delivery proposition? What role can the Intranet play? What role can the Extranet play?
- Is the business strategy to meet customer values by achieving operational excellence, customer intimacy, or technical superiority?

The strategy choice of operational excellence, customer intimacy, or technical superiority will drive entirely different e-business initiatives and strategies. For example, a business that is striving for operational efficiency will utilize e-business for areas such as e-procurement, supply chain integration, customer self-service, employee communications, and online recruiting. A business that is striving for customer intimacy will utilize e-business for customer support, customer surveys and input, personalized marketing, portals, building communities, and automating the contact center. A business striving for technical superiority will utilize e-business for engineering, interfacing with CAD, communicating with suppliers, and reducing the time-to-market.

Building networked business models to create maximum value will be critical in the future. Consider the business strategy relative to suppliers, partners, and other stakeholders:

- With what partners and suppliers will the business need to align?
- How can the business build trust and share among partners?
- What is the true core identity of the business? Disassemble or outsource those activities not core, assemble those that are core. What can be separated or outsourced?
- What is the business doing that it should not be doing?

Now that the e-business strategy has been designed from the outside in, go back to the business plan and review the business mission, vision, values, objectives, and strategies to determine if it requires updating. Not all business models will be equally impacted by the Internet. For example, if the company is based on a service (e.g., cutting hair, restaurant), the Internet can facilitate or enhance the delivery of the service, but will probably not replace it. However, if the industry is heavily information based (e.g., insurance, banking, finance, publishing, education, travel management, lead management), the industry may be more significantly impacted by the Internet and other technologies. There are many other factors that can influence the impact the Internet will have, including number of competitors, ease of entry into the market, costs, and demand. Therefore, the e-business strategy may significantly impact the original business plan, or affect it very little.

Make sure the business focus and priorities are very clear. Efficiency, costs, profits, and customer satisfaction cannot be of equal importance to the organization. The organization cannot have it all in the new value-driven economy. For example, if the organization's true priority is customer satisfaction, the organization may have to link with competitors and partners even at the expense of profits and trade secrets.

The following are questions to help in reviewing the business plan impact:

- **Mission:** A mission is a clear, concise, informative, and compelling statement of the company's purpose. Has e-business changed what the company does, what groups of customers are served, what products or services are provided, or what sets the business apart from competition?

- **Vision:** A vision is an inspiring statement that identifies where the company is going and what it is going to become. Has e-business changed where the company is going or what it is going to become? Remember, although ambitious words motivate, impossible words discourage. There is a thin line between a vision and a hallucination; make sure it is grounded in reality.
- **Values:** Values are a set of beliefs and principles used to guide actions. Has e-business and designing the strategy from the outside in changed how the company wants to articulate the values?
- **Goals:** Goals are the plan to reach the mission. They are broad business results that the business is committed to achieving. Goals link the mission to daily activities. Goals are discussed below in the Metrics section. Do the goals need to change in light of thinking from the outside in? What are the short- and long-term business goals (e.g., increase market share, improve customer service, improve business to business, improve coordination among departments, increase efficiency and reduce costs, increase employee satisfaction/retention/recruitment)? Goals generally involve enhancing revenue, reducing costs, or improving customer service. Do the goals align with the strategic focus and direction?
- **Objectives:** Objectives are steps necessary to take to achieve the goals. Objectives are specific, measurable, attainable, and time-based. Do these objectives change as a result of e-business? Are the stated levels of ambition, goals, and objectives high enough or do they need to be reset? Can the objectives be accomplished more quickly with the e-business initiatives?

Are the business plan statements consistent with the e-business strategy? For example, if a company is planning to use e-business to achieve customer intimacy, that should be the main driver in the business mission, vision, values, and objectives rather than operational excellence or technical superiority. As mentioned earlier, an e-business strategy and initiatives to support customer intimacy would be drastically different from operational excellence or technical superiority. If the strategies and direction are inconsistent or unclear, the organization will be confused and unfocused. With a confused focus, e-business ventures may not provide the company the competitive advantage or return that is anticipated. For example, Apple Computer's vision has been "To change the world through technology." From that vision, it would be very clear that Apple strives for technical superiority and the e-business strategy should support the technical product development.

Now draft the strategy section of your e-business plan document.

METRICS

Now that the strategy has been identified, how does the business measure progress against that strategy? To answer that question, define how the business will measure value in the future. Many companies measure progress only with internal financial metrics such as sales, profits, return on investment, or costs. Companies that manage based upon a balanced scorecard have customer and people metrics as part of their measures in addition to financial metrics. The balanced scorecard is a more accurate representation as it recognizes that no single measure can provide a clear picture of how an organization is functioning. Although it is important to have financial, internal, and people metrics, a customer-driven organization that has developed the strategy from the outside in should emphasize customer metrics.

Identifying specific metrics to measure the success of e-business initiatives can be a challenge. One company identified the business impact that e-business would have on the organization, as follows:

■ Reduced calls to customer support as customers would obtain information from the Internet
■ Customer satisfaction should increase as customers are able to obtain information and have individual preferences and needs addressed
■ Customer retention would increase through improved customer service
■ Business processes should be faster and less expensive as information and processes are facilitated by the Internet
■ Supplier costs would decrease as a result of streamlining the business process and improved relationships
■ New customers would be attracted through faster time-to-market and value-added services
■ Sales would increase through self-service order processing, up-selling, and cross-selling
■ Overall business and profit should grow as well as market reach and recognition

Some companies identify specific business metrics that would be impacted by e-business, such as:

■ Customer satisfaction will increase
■ Number of repeat customers will increase
■ Customer responsiveness will increase
■ Customer retention will increase
■ Customer complaints will decrease

- Number of returns will decrease
- Number of customer support calls will decrease
- Average cost per call (revenue/calls) will decrease
- Cost per order (sales/order) will decrease
- Cash-to-cash cycle time will decrease (includes days of inventory, days of receivable, days payable, production cycle time, and days sales outstanding)
- Number of customers will increase
- Sales will increase
- Number of partners will increase
- Supplier responsiveness will increase
- Total costs will decrease
- Productivity will increase
- Profits will increase
- Cost of marketing (marketing/revenue) will decrease
- Market share will increase
- Quality of order fulfillment will increase
- Documentation accuracy will increase

The problem with measuring e-business success with either the business effect or business metric method is that there may be no way to isolate a direct correlation between the result and the e-business initiative. If the Internet is used to generate sales, Internet sales can be measured. However, a company may utilize the Internet for more indirect benefits such as promotion, customer service, or increasing customer satisfaction. For example, if sales increased, perhaps it was not due to the new e-business functionality, but rather new product design, an aggressive marketing campaign, or many other business initiatives that are occurring at the same time.

Other companies measure e-business by technical metrics, such as:

- Number of hits to the Internet, number of page views, site traffic
- Areas of the site most visited, paths visitors took within the site, click-through rates (number of successive screens a visitor goes through)
- Duration, number of minutes per average user on the site
- Number of Internet transactions processed, number of inquiries satisfied by Internet hits, number of self-service interactions
- Abandonment rates, abandonment rates with items in shopping cart
- Percent of visitors who return within a year, time between visits, customer loyalty, customer retention rate (by purchases)
- Percent of visitors who are buyers, reach (percentage of visitors who are potential buyers), number of new visitors to the Internet site, visitors by country

- Interest percent (any action expressing interest, registering, asking for information)
- Number of proactive touches with a customer
- Mean time between failures, availability time, mean time to repair, server and site up-time, load balancing statistics, page and form errors
- End-to-end response time average, throughput time, page load time
- Number of security issues, resistance to assault or intrusions
- Length of time since last update of site information
- Dollars spent on e-business

The difficulty in utilizing the technical metrics is that there is no tie from the usage to the business value that was generated as a result of the usage. For example, just because the organization had 10M visitors to the site, did that help profits increase?

There are two possible options to address the cause-and-effect dilemma when measuring e-business success:

- Utilize a balanced scorecard approach with the business metrics as well as the technical metrics. The true picture is a combination of the two types of metrics. This balanced approach shows that there are various indicators that need to be considered in total to determine the progress. Be sure not to utilize too many metrics, but rather just a few of the ones key to the business strategy. Exhibit 5.1 shows an example of a balanced e-business scorecard used at one company.
- The measurement of e-business success could be simplified to one metric, that of customer satisfaction. An organization that is driven by the customer and has developed the strategy from the outside in has only one true measure of success, that of customer satisfaction. For example, an Internet site providing information could have an occasional pop-up window that asks the customer to rate his/her satisfaction with the Internet page in providing the information needed. The customer could be rewarded with a discount for replying to the survey.

The following questions can assist in developing metrics to measure success:

- Review the value proposition. What do the customers and business value?
- How can that value be measured?
- What are the desired effects of e-business on the organization?

Exhibit 5.1 E-Business Balanced Scorecard

Financial:
- Percent of e-business projects delivered within budget
- Return on e-business investment
- Total e-business budget vs. actual total budget amount
- Online sales dollars
- Percentage of total revenue generated online
- Cost to process an order
- Cash-to-cash cycle time

Customer:
- Number of visitors
- Interest percent (visitors taking action, registering)
- Conversion rate from visitor to buyer
- Percent of visitors returning within a year
- Time between visits
- Duration of visits
- Satisfaction
- Percent market share

Internal Process:
- Abandonment rates
- Time to respond to a customer
- Number of proactive touches with a customer per month
- Inventory levels and turns
- Site up-time, availability
- Site response throughput time, page load time
- Number of security issues, intrusions

People:
- Time of e-business project from concept to implementation
- Length of time since last major content update

Now draft the metrics section of your e-business plan document.
Now that the value proposition, strategy, and metrics have been developed, you are ready to define the specific e-business opportunities that will help the business achieve the strategy.

KEY POINTS TO REMEMBER

■ Success in the new economy is dependent upon a company concisely establishing its core competencies and value proposition. Select what the company does best and outsource the rest.

■ The value delivery proposition has the potential to totally change the industry or to create a new industry.

- The business plan and the e-business strategy must complement each other and be consistent.
- The business strategy of operational excellence, customer intimacy, or technical superiority will drive entirely different e-business initiatives and strategies.
- Building networked business models to create maximum value will be critical in the future.
- Utilize a balanced scorecard approach to measuring e-business success with business metrics as well as technical metrics.
- The true measurement of e-business success is customer satisfaction.

NOTES FOR MY E-BUSINESS EFFORT

_____

_____

_____

_____

_____

_____

_____

_____

_____

_____

_____

_____

_____

_____

_____

_____

_____

_____

_____

_____

_____

_____

6

PHASE 4—DEFINE

"The problem is never how to get new, innovative thoughts in your mind, but how to get the old ones out."

Dee Hock

The fourth phase of the e-business planning process is **Define**. As Figure 6.1 shows, in this phase you will define the e-business opportunities, assess the competitive situation, and define the e-business priorities. At the end of this phase, you will have completed the following sections in the e-business plan document:

- Opportunities
- Competitive Situation

OPPORTUNITIES

Identifying opportunities can be fun as it is a time to be creative and think outside of the box. It is best done in group brainstorming sessions with both business and technical individuals present. Identify opportunities by going back to the list of stakeholders and the stakeholder processes that were identified earlier. Also go back to the value proposition that you identified. Ask the key statement as shown in Figure 6.2:

For each stakeholder and each step of his/her process, what can the company do specifically to meet the value statements identified?

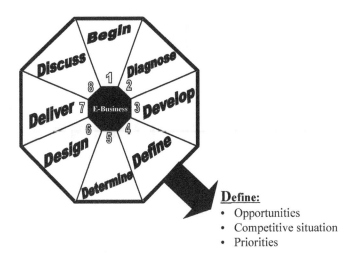

Define:
- Opportunities
- Competitive situation
- Priorities

Figure 6.1   Phase 4, Define

Opportunity Identification

For each stakeholder and each step of his/her process, what can the company do to meet the value statements identified?

Figure 6.2   Opportunity Identification

For example, for a hearing-aid manufacturer, the end patient was iden-tified as one of the stakeholders. The process used by the patient was to:

- Recognize the need: the patient's hearing loss is severe enough to warrant a solution
- Determine where to go for care
- Determine the specific product to purchase

- Purchase the product and get fitted
- Obtain service and support

The value that the hearing-aid manufacturer wanted to provide was to:

- Provide knowledge and promote learning
- Focus on the preferences and needs of individuals
- Simplify the ease of doing business
- Provide hearing solutions

So, to identify the opportunities, ask the group: When a patient is recognizing the need for a hearing aid, what can the company do to provide information, focus on individual needs, simplify the ease of doing business, and provide hearing solutions? Ideas such as the following could be generated:

- Provide general industry information on technology, product types, functionality, and cost range
- Provide a self-diagnostic process that assists patients in determining needs for hearing aids
- Provide symptoms and warning signs of a hearing loss
- Provide information on anatomy of the ear, how hearing works, and how a hearing aid can help
- Identify causes and types of hearing impairment
- Identify benefits of better hearing, including binaural vs. mononaural (one or two hearing aids)
- Provide information targeted to patient niches and demographics (e.g., kids, veterans)
- Provide information on common misconceptions about hearing aids
- Provide complete information on the entire process of obtaining a hearing aid
- Provide general information on purchasing products including insurance and financial assistance
- Provide comments from other patients who have obtained hearing aids, what it was like to go through the process, testimonials. What are the benefits?
- Provide a forum for the patient to communicate with professionals or other patients
- Provide pointers to other portals on the Internet to go for hearing-related information
- Capture the names and addresses of visitors and proactively market hearing solutions to them one-on-one. For example: "Hi, Mildred, thank you for visiting our site today. We notice from your responses

on the hearing questions that you may have a slight hearing difficulty. Although your hearing may be normal, you may want to investigate your hearing situation further. Click here to find the professional nearest you for assistance in learning more about how we can improve your life."

■ Provide frequently asked questions and answers in this step of the process
■ Provide the ability to contact the right person within the company who can help in this step of the process (contact us, but specific not generic). This could include online assistance.

Go through this opportunity generation process for each stakeholder and each step of the stakeholder's process. You will be amazed at how many opportunities you can generate in this structured approach. Don't be surprised if hundreds of opportunities are identified. Don't be alarmed; all the opportunities may not be implemented. Opportunities will be prioritized in a subsequent step. Rather than random opportunities, the opportunities will all support the value that the customer desires. This demonstrates how the planning process is generated from the outside in, from the customer perspective.

In addition to generating many opportunities, this process will also actually organize the flow of the Web site functionality. The best way to organize Web functionality is in the process and order in which the information will be accessed and utilized. This is the exact way in which opportunities have been identified—by the customer process. It may make sense to organize the Web site functionality by the type of stakeholder. For example, the end-customer needs may be different from those of a distributor, which may be different from those of the general public. Within the type of stakeholder, the functionality can be organized by the process the stakeholder will use.

Although most stakeholders will have a process, a few of the stakeholder groups, such as the public and the employees, may not have a defined process, but rather groups of information needs. For example, the general public may have the following information needs:

■ Language choice
■ Overview of the company; identify what the company does, the size, locations, markets, industry, etc.
■ Overview of the products and services
■ Locations, including directions from airports, hotel information
■ History of the company
■ Local charities and community action
■ Careers and job openings

- News releases
- Company strategy, vision, direction, and plans
- Company events and calendar
- How to contact the company, including online assistance
- Frequently asked questions and answers
- Site search
- Site map

These information needs will also become opportunities. Employee information needs may include both company and departmental information, such as:

- **Company:** Provide information that builds an understanding of the company, its direction, current initiatives, and activities.
  - Business plan including roadmap, goals and objectives, and current status
  - Organizational information, roles and responsibilities
  - Phone directory and contact lists
  - Job postings
  - Corporate communications including internal announcements, investigations, expansions, changes, company news, press releases, presentations, Web conferences
  - Newsletters
  - Corporate calendar (holidays, fiscal calendar)
  - Information on sports leagues and events
  - Company store
  - Report on profit-sharing scorecard
  - Report on company scorecards and key metrics
  - Competitive information, comparisons and market data
  - Frequently asked questions and answers about the company
  - The ability to contact the right person within the company who can help (contact us, but specific not generic)
- **Departmental:** The following criteria and guidelines will be used in designing information content for each department:
  - Department information, including description, mission, and organization
  - Department direction including roadmap, metrics, projects, project status, and updates
  - Departmental communication, including presentations, information, documentation, guidelines, policies and procedures, process flowcharts, work instructions, product-related information, training, schedules and events
  - Departmental forms and templates

— Downloads
— Troubleshooting and frequently asked questions related to the department
— Published reports and online queries
— Search functionality
— Portal to departmental-related Web links
— Contact ability, including the ability to provide suggestions and improvements for the department, requests, ability to contact the right person within the department (including paging ability if necessary)

As shown in Figure 6.3, depending upon the stakeholder, the opportunities may be for the Internet, Extranet, or Intranet. For example, employees may be Intranet opportunities. End customers or the public may be Internet opportunities. Suppliers or distributors may be Extranet opportunities. Identify each opportunity as Internet, Extranet, or Intranet capabilities.

Now draft the opportunity section of the e-business plan document for each of the stakeholders that were identified.

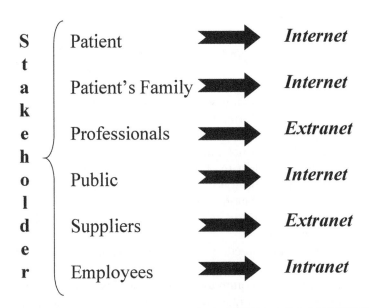

Figure 6.3 Identify Internet, Extranet, or Intranet

COMPETITIVE SITUATION

In Phase 2 (Chapter 4), the industry in general and the value chain were diagnosed. Now that potential opportunities have been identified, it is a good time to take a closer look at each of the competitors in detail. After this detailed analysis, the true competitive advantages can be identified. It is amazing how much can be learned about competitors by a thorough review of their Web sites! The Internet provides an excellent vehicle to evaluate competition, better than any means used in the past.

Take each opportunity that was identified in the previous step and enter it into a spreadsheet. It is also helpful to include the stakeholder and process step for informational and sorting purposes. Include a column for each of the major competitors. Try to keep the list to six to eight competitors so it is manageable. Go to competitors' sites and rate them on a scale of 0 to 5:

5: The competitor provides significant functionality for this opportunity, content is excellent

4: The competitor provides above average functionality for this opportunity, very good content

3: The competitor provides average functionality and content for this opportunity

2: The competitor provides below average functionality and content

1: The competitor provides shallow functionality and content, but something does exist

0: Nothing exists for this opportunity

After grading the competitors' performances on the opportunities, it is time to grade your company's current site functionality using the same criteria. Figure 6.4 shows an example of a portion of a competitive matrix.

You will probably be able to grade only the Internet opportunities as you would not have access to compare the Intranet and Extranet functionality. As you go through the competitor sites, you might also identify some additional opportunities to add to the list.

As Figure 6.5 shows, the findings for all the companies may be summarized by:

■ Totaling the points for each company. In general, the totals should identify which companies had the best to worst Internet functionalities.

■ Counting the number of opportunities for each company that were addressed with some functionality (had a score greater than zero). This total indicates the **breadth** of the company's functionality.

Number	Internet Opportunity	Stakeholder	Process	Competitor A	Competitor B	Competitor C	Competitor D	Us
1	Provide general industry information on technology, product types, functionality, and cost range.	Patient	Recognizing the need	3	3	2		
2	Provide a self-diagnostic process that assists patients in determining needs for hearing aids.	Patient	Recognizing the need					5
3	Provide symptoms and warning signs of a hearing loss.	Patient	Recognizing the need	2	4	2	2	2
4	Provide information on anatomy of the ear, how hearing works, and how a hearing aid can help.	Patient	Recognizing the need	4	5	2	3	1
5	Identify causes and types of hearing impairment.	Patient	Recognizing the need	2	4	1	3	
6	Identify benefits of better hearing, including mononaural vs. binaural (one or two hearing aids).	Patient	Recognizing the need		2	2	1	
7	Provide information targeted to patient niches and demographics (e.g., children, veterans).	Patient	Recognizing the need		3			2
8	Provide information on common misconceptions about hearing aids.	Patient	Recognizing the need					3
9	Provide complete information on the entire process of obtaining a hearing aid.	Patient	Recognizing the need		2		1	
10	Provide general information on purchasing products including insurance and financial assistance.	Patient	Recognizing the need					
11	Provide comments from other patients who have obtained hearing aids, what it was like to go through the process, testimonials. What are the benefits?	Patient	Recognizing the need		5			
12	Provide a forum for the patient to communicate with professionals or other patients.	Patient	Recognizing the need					
13	Provide pointers to other portals on the Internet to go to for hearing-related information.	Patient	Recognizing the need	1	2		1	3
14	Capture the names and addresses of visitors and proactively market hearing solutions to them one-on-one.	Patient	Recognizing the need					1
15	Provide frequently asked questions and answers in this step of the process.	Patient	Recognizing the need					
16	Provide the ability to contact the right person within the company who can help in this step of the process (contact us, but specific not generic). This could include online assistance.	Patient	Recognizing the need					

Figure 6.4   Competitive Matrix

Number	Internet Opportunity	Stakeholder	Process	Competitor A	Competitor B	Competitor C	Competitor D	Us
	TOTAL			54	67	45	60	41
	Count (Breadth)			17	20	17	24	21
	Average (Depth)			3.2	3.4	2.6	2.5	2.0
	Gap (Opportunity)			61	58	61	54	57

Figure 6.5   Competitive Summary

- Averaging the total score divided by the count. This average indicates the **depth** of the functionality for each opportunity for which the company had functionality.
- Calculating the **gap**, or competitive opportunity, for each company by subtracting the count from the total number of opportunities that were possible. This indicates the opportunity for improvement.

It can be extremely interesting to review the totals and findings. For example, if a company has a high number for depth and a low number in the count row, what the company does, it does very well. The following questions will guide the analysis:

- What was learned from a detailed review of competitor Web sites?
- Which company had the best site? Which had the worst site? Does this make sense when you consider what is known about the companies?
- Overall, how did your company's site compare to the competitors' sites?
- Which competitors had the greatest breadth, or addressed the most opportunities?
- Which competitors had the greatest depth and content?
- How many opportunities had no competitor addressed? Review these for potential competitive advantages.
- Which stakeholders had the most complete scores? For example, were the majority of ratings for the public higher than the ratings for the end customer? It may be an opportunity to more thoroughly address the needs for a particular stakeholder.
- Which process steps had the weakest scores? For example, was more functionality provided in recognizing the need than in service and support? It may be an opportunity to more thoroughly address the needs for a particular step in the process.
- What is the unique functionality that is covered today? What opportunities were addressed by just one company?

- What are the opportunities that no company covers today?
- How did navigation and screen design compare for each company?
- What companies had worldwide and language capabilities?
- Did it appear that any of the companies had Extranet functionality or areas that were restricted to members only by the use of an ID and password?
- What percent of the opportunities did no company address? How much opportunity is there to create a unique competitive differentiation in the market?
- What new opportunities were identified? How can one-to-one marketing be developed? How can customer loyalty be increased?
- Do you want to copy a successful competitor or re-invent the industry?

An example of a competitive summary overview is shown in Exhibit 6.1.
Now draft the competitive situation section of your e-business plan document.

PRIORITIES

It is important to prioritize the opportunities that were identified as this step will take time and resources to implement each opportunity. There is a limit to the amount of time and resources that a company can spend on e-business initiatives, and clear priorities ensure completion in the best order as defined by the business. Priorities cannot be finalized until the complete impact on the application architecture, technical architecture, people, and processes is identified as this impact will determine the costs and impact the return on investment. However, it is a good time to begin to categorize and sort the opportunities into groupings or projects and obtain some initial thoughts on priorities. It is important that the business or customers—not the Information Systems organization—prioritize the opportunities. The business or customers say what to build and Information Systems identifies how to build it.

Following are seven ways to begin to prioritize the opportunities, as shown in Figure 6.6:

1. Stage of evolution
2. Balanced portfolio
3. Business opportunity
4. Ease of deployment
5. Business value
6. Forced ranking
7. Customer driven

Exhibit 6.1   Competitive Summary Description

Competitive Summary

- The best overall site was Competitor B (rating total of 67 points), followed by Competitor D (60 points), Competitor A (54), and Competitor C (45), with our company the lowest-rated site with 41 points.
- Competitor B had depth as well as breadth. It covered 20 opportunities of a total of 78 for a total of 67 points, or 3.4 average rating.
- Competitor A had deep functionality and content, but covered fewer items. In other words, what it did, it did well. It covered only 17 opportunities, but had 54 total points, for an average of 3.2.
- Our content was very shallow. The average was 2.0.
- All companies covered very similar functionality, or opportunities, on their public sites (although depth varied somewhat).
- Although each competitor had a few unique opportunities, similar opportunities were covered to some degree. The unique opportunities included:
  - Self-diagnostic hearing test
  - Misconceptions about hearing aids
  - Testimonials from patients who have obtained a hearing aid
  - Capturing names and addresses of patients taking a hearing test
  - Information on various hearing technologies with advantages and disadvantages
  - Information on warranties
  - Information on adjusting to life with a hearing aid
  - Information on caring for a hearing aid
  - Common problems or questions about the hearing aid
  - Information on where customers can go for service worldwide
  - Operating instructions
- In general, no companies served the patient and provided much assistance for the patient during the purchase and get fitted stages or the service and support stages. This could provide a market advantage if we are able to provide significant functionally in these areas.
- No companies designed the navigation from the customer viewpoint. Navigation was often confusing and information was difficult to find.
- Competitors A and B demonstrated their worldwide abilities by providing their pages in international languages.
- It was not obvious from the Internet site if any of the companies had an Extranet targeted at professionals (e.g., button for professionals or patients to enter with ID and password).

Exhibit 6.1   Competitive Summary Description (continued)

Competitive Summary

■ Using the e-business evolution chart, the industry is relatively immature, or at its beginning use of the Internet. The main use is for informational purposes (with a total of 194 points), with only 22 points in the service category, 0 points in the transactional category, 39 points in the interaction category, and 12 in the community category.

■ There is a tremendous opportunity for us as the highest that any one competitor scored was 31% (24 out of the 78 opportunities identified). There is definitely room to create a unique competitive differentiation in the market.

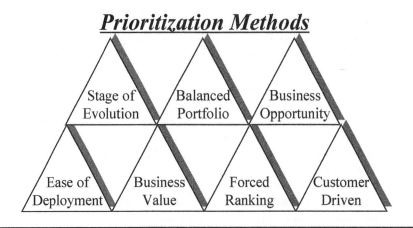

Figure 6.6   Prioritization Methods

Each of these methods will be described in detail. You may choose to utilize one, all, or some combination of these methods to determine priorities. The prioritization method must fit the company and the personalities of executive management.

1.   Stage of Evolution Prioritization

Figure 6.7 identifies the typical stages of e-business evolution that a company may go through. The stages of evolution include:

■ **Information:** This is the first stage of e-business evolution where the company obtains a web page and simply displays information about the company. This may include brochure-ware and marketing information with an overview of the company, a history of the company, and a financial summary of the company. It typically

E-Business Evolution

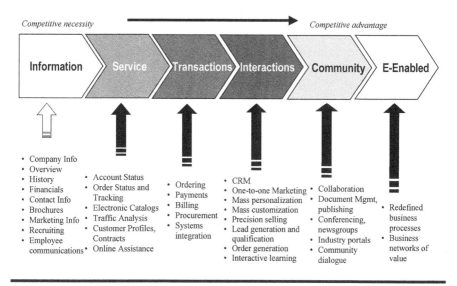

Figure 6.7   E-Business Evolution

includes contact and location information as well as recruiting information. The Intranet may include basic employee communications information and employee phone directories. Essentially, the Internet is a tool for one-way publishing at this stage of evolution.

■ **Service:** The second stage, service, is where the company begins to have a dialog with customers. It typically provides accounts status, order status, and tracking information. It may include catalog information and basic price list information. Customer profile and contract information is stored, and the company is able to provide online assistance.

■ **Transactions:** Next, the company typically moves into processing transactions. This may include taking orders, processing invoices, and payments. Procurement may also be done through the Internet. Front-end and back-end systems are beginning to become integrated.

■ **Interactions:** In this stage, the company actually begins to proactively interact with the customer. Typically, Customer Relationship Management (CRM) systems are integrated with the Internet to enhance one-to-one relationships and manage lead generation and qualification. The focus is on personalization, customization, and precision selling. Customer profiles are even more robust and handle contract and customized pricing. Orders are proactively generated. Interactive learning is also utilized in this stage of evolution.

- **Community:** Next, the organization provides communities of interest by linking interested parties together for collaboration. Industry portals, community dialogue, conferencing, and newsgroups are all ways to facilitate community. Partners within a value chain are closely linked and share information such as document management.
- **E-Enabled:** When the enterprise is e-enabled, all business processes are redefined and enabled with Internet technology. Although many of the key business processes may be redesigned in previous stages, in this stage all business processes are redesigned and Internet enabled. The entire business network of value is automated and integrated for efficiency.

It is interesting to note that as a company progresses through the stages of evolution, the efforts migrate from competitive necessity at the early stages to more of a competitive advantage at the later stages of the evolution. The investment, risk, complexity, and skill requirements also increase as a company moves from the early stages to the later stages of e-business evolution. The type of opportunities to the left of the evolution diagram are typically easy to implement as they are more informational driven. The opportunities that are easier to implement are typically focused on operational efficiency and have a lower overall competitive advantage to and impact on the business. Opportunities to the right of the evolution diagram are typically new and innovative to the market and industry with a high business impact and opportunity. These opportunities would provide more of a competitive advantage and create more value, increase market growth, and enhance revenues. To prioritize by the stage of evolution:

- Identify each opportunity by stage in which it occurs: Informational, Service, Transactions, Interactions, Community, or E-Enabled.
- Sort the list of opportunities by stage.

After identifying the stage of evolution for each opportunity, go back to the competitive analysis and competitive matrix completed earlier. In what stage of e-business evolution are the general industry and competitors? Calculate this by adding the number of points for the opportunities classified in each stage. For example, one company found its industry to have 194 points in the informational stage, 22 points in the service stage, 0 in the transactional, 39 in the interaction, and 12 in the community. In general, this industry is in the immature or early stages of e-business, and there would be a significant opportunity in the market.

2. Balanced Portfolio Prioritization

The balanced portfolio is similar to the first prioritization method, Stage of Evolution. However, the result is different. After classifying the opportunities by stage of evolution, this method is based on the premise that a company should have a balanced portfolio of e-business initiatives. As stated earlier, as the stages progress, the risk, investment, difficulty, and competitive opportunity also increase. Therefore, the development portfolio should include one opportunity from each phase of the development stage to balance the risk, investment, and opportunity.

3. Business Opportunity Prioritization

To prioritize by business opportunity, go back to the competitive analysis completed. Review the opportunities that only a few competitors or no competitors addressed. These opportunities would be the top priority as they are the most innovative and unique to the industry. Rank each opportunity on a scale of 0 to 5 in terms of the competitive advantage it could provide. A "5" would provide a significant competitive advantage, "3" would be average, and "0" would be no competitive advantage.

4. Ease of Deployment Prioritization

This prioritization method is based on the principle of addressing the low hanging fruit first. Rate each opportunity on a scale of 1 to 5 on ease of implementing. A "5" would indicate that it would be very easy. Consider both the technical development effort as well as the business process changes that are necessary. Typically, the informational opportunities would fall into this category as they would be largely content driven rather than requiring programming or interfacing to back-end systems. A "1" would indicate very difficult to implement and would perhaps require additional tools, infrastructure, or skill set. Address the easier priorities first ("5") and build the skill set and infrastructure as the company moves to the more difficult opportunities.

5. Business Value Prioritization

The premise of this prioritization method is that the opportunities should be prioritized by the business value or business objectives. Go back to the value proposition that was created in Phase 3 (Chapter 5). Weigh the values on how important they are to the success of the business on a scale of 5 to 10. A higher number indicates that the value significantly impacts the organization. Next, for each opportunity, identify the opportunity's impact for each value on a scale of 1 to 10. If the company implements this opportunity, what impact will it have on this particular value? Then, multiply the importance weight times the impact value to get a weighted number. For example, if the value was to provide information, and it was weighed a "6," and the opportunity was to provide information on how hearing works, the impact would be an "8." The weighted number would be "48." Total all the numbers. The opportunities with the higher scores would be a higher priority as they would have a greater impact on the business.

6. Forced Ranking Prioritization

Forced ranking is a process where the group votes on which of any two opportunities would be more beneficial. With the project team, this process should be completed quickly and with little discussion. Compare the first opportunity with the second, then the first opportunity with the third, fourth, fifth, through the entire list. Then compare the second opportunity with the third, fourth, fifth, and so on. Ask the project team to vote. If they could have only one of the two opportunities, which would they choose? The project with the most votes gets a mark. The participants need to vote objectively for what would be best for the customer and company. Add up all the marks for each opportunity. List the opportunities in descending order based on the marks for a prioritized list.

7. Customer-Driven Prioritization

For a true customer-driven strategy, the opportunities should be prioritized by the customer. Having the customer prioritize the opportunities results in a design and roadmap that are definitely driven from the outside-in. To do this, group all the informational opportunities from the Stage of Evolution prioritization method. Also, group all opportunities that are easy to do from the Ease of Deployment prioritization method. The point is that the informational opportunities and those easy to do should just be done, as they require little work or investment, and it would take more time to ask the customer than it would be worth. Now the more difficult opportunities remain. Have the customers prioritize these opportunities on a scale of 1 to 5, with the higher number indicating the greater value the opportunity would provide them. This could be done in a number of different ways:

- Have an online survey that customers complete and get something in return for their time.
- Form a customer focus group that would prioritize the opportunities.

Each stakeholder would prioritize his/her opportunities. For example, the customer would prioritize customer opportunities and the supplier would prioritize the supplier opportunities.

Congratulations, you have now identified opportunities that support the e-business strategy, reviewed the competitive situation, and have an initial priority list of the opportunities!

KEY POINTS TO REMEMBER

■ To identify opportunities, go back to the stakeholders, the stakeholders' processes, and the business value statements that were identified previously. Ask: For each stakeholder and each step of the stakeholder process, what can the company do specifically to meet the value statements identified?

■ Review each competitor's site, and rate how well each competitor achieves each opportunity. Summarize the results.

■ Prioritize opportunities based on stage of evolution, balanced portfolio, business opportunity, ease of deployment, business value, forced ranking, and a customer-driven method.

NOTES FOR MY E-BUSINESS EFFORT

_____

_____

_____

_____

_____

_____

_____

_____

_____

_____

_____

_____

_____

_____

_____

_____

_____

_____

_____

_____

_____

_____

_____

_____

7

PHASE 5—DETERMINE

"We can't solve problems by using the same kind of thinking we used when we created them."

Albert Einstein

The fifth phase of the e-business planning process is to **Determine**. In previous phases, you have defined the strategy and e-business opportunities. As shown in Figure 7.1, in this phase, you will determine the impact of this new direction on the application architecture, technical architecture, people/organization, information systems, and business processes. You will also determine the cost/benefit analysis and roadmap for implementation. In this phase, you will complete the e-business plan and obtain approval for the design and delivery of the e-business plan. This phase completes the planning stage, while Phases 6 through 8 will focus on execution. At the end of this phase, you will complete the following sections in the e-business plan document:

- Business Application
- Technical Infrastructure
- Business Processes
- Information Systems Processes
- People/Organization
- Costs
- Benefits
- Return on Investment (ROI)
- Roadmap
- Executive Summary

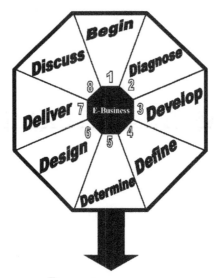

Determine:

- Application architecture impact
- Technical architecture impact
- Business process impact
- IS process impact
- People/organization impact
- Cost/benefit analysis
- Roadmap
- Approval

Figure 7.1 Phase 5, Determine

APPLICATION ARCHITECTURE IMPACT

E-business can have a significant impact on the business applications architecture. In order to compete in the future collaborative marketplace, companies need flexible and integrated business applications. Moving to a customer-centric strategy will drive information systems to focus on an overall information infrastructure. Integration of applications will become critical. To be a truly e-enabled organization, all the business applications from front-end to back-end must be fully integrated to provide:

- Immediate on-line information
- Accurate information
- Information in one place

■ Business flexibility and agility
■ Automated workflow

The business applications in many companies are not ready for a direct interface to customers. Many application systems were not designed to operate in concert, exchange data seamlessly, operate at Internet speed, or use a common database. Selling a product quickly over the Internet, and then dealing with an unintegrated and unresponsive legacy fulfillment mechanism is a sure way to lose customers. Some companies attempt to implement e-business without first addressing the core business applications. Perhaps they have not implemented Enterprise Requirements Planning (ERP) and have islands of disparate applications and information. Although these companies can successfully add some of the e-business functionality, it is impossible to get to a complete e-enabled enterprise without having an enterprise framework of business applications. ERP and an enterprise application framework allow the business to organize accurate information, and the Internet allows the organization to communicate this information directly to the customer. Without an enterprise framework of business applications, independent applications result in:

■ **A significant reduction in flexibility.** Whenever a business change occurs, many programs and databases may need to be altered as the logic and information could be redundant. Any point where disparate systems require interfacing and integration is typically a weak link that requires additional attention. If information systems projects and changes take months and years rather than weeks due to the redundancy and integration requirements, a business cannot keep pace with the quickly changing market and customer demands.

■ **A significant increase in cost.** Each of the islands of information and processing logic must be modified as changes occur. It is more costly to maintain something in multiple places than in one place.

■ **A decrease in accuracy due to redundancy.** Whenever there are islands of information, the question is raised as to which database contains the accurate information. One organization may have ten different databases of customer information as seen by the various silos of the organization. Usually none of the databases is accurate. Inaccurate data often lead to customer dissatisfaction.

■ **An increase in processing time.** In e-business there is no option other than to provide real-time information immediately. Waiting an additional second for a transaction to process can be noticed by the customer. With independent applications that have fragile

Level of Application Development

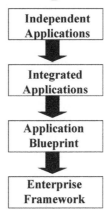

Figure 7.2 Level of Application Development

bridges and interfaces, batch processing, and redundant data structures, transaction time will increase.

Figure 7.2 identifies how an organization must move down the scale from independent applications to integrated applications, to an application blueprint, and finally to an enterprise framework of business applications to be successful at e-business. Although a business can add e-business functionality to independent applications, it is much like putting perfume on a pig: you may disguise the stench for a while, but it is still there! An enterprise framework allows an organization to put substance behind its Web site.

Although it may seem like a daunting task to move the applications down the evolution to an enterprise framework, it can be completed over time. All the business applications do not need to be e-enabled at the same time, but can occur in phases. Tools are available to help begin the integration while the business looks at building an integrated enterprise framework. Some of these tools include Enterprise Application Integration tools, interface adapters, or message brokers (e.g., IBM MQSeries or XML-based Data Junction). While moving to an enterprise framework, companies need to build interfaces wisely as more layers of integration will increase the complexity and maintenance of a solution.

Look at the entire application architecture for the company, and ask the following questions:

- What information architecture is needed to support the requirements?
- What application architecture is needed to support the e-business model and customer requirements?
- What applications require integration to be successful?
- What application modules must be e-enabled, and what is the relative priority?
- Which applications contribute significantly to the business and which ones require disproportionate support?
- What applications can be directly connected to customers in order to improve the flow?
- How can e-mail interactions with customers be automated?
- How can e-mail, phone, and Internet interactions be integrated?
- How can the various customer touch-points be integrated?
- What information should be available to better support the business decisions?
- What applications can be directly connected to suppliers in order to improve the flow?
- How can a closer interface be obtained with suppliers and the value chain to forecast demand and schedule more accurately?
- How can costs be decreased?
- Does the organization have a common language, definitions, rules, goals, and commitment? What are the business hurdles?
- Does the organization have any issues doing business without any boundaries (e.g., sales territories, plants, countries, languages, or cultures)?
- For e-business to succeed, what impact or coordination will be required with the parent company, sister companies, divisions, distribution channel, suppliers, and partners?

Figure 7.3 shows the high-level application framework for one company. Figure 7.4 identifies the same framework in a little more detail. This framework was utilized with business management to identify which blocks of the enterprise application framework should be automated and integrated first. The company was able to prioritize which building blocks to work on first.

The business application framework for each company may be slightly different depending on the company's business, markets, and competitive strengths. After identifying the framework, each building block of the e-business applications can be further defined, such as:

- **E-Marketing:** The purpose of e-marketing is to create an effective marketing relationship between the company and its customers. The Internet provides an entirely new marketing channel. The focus is

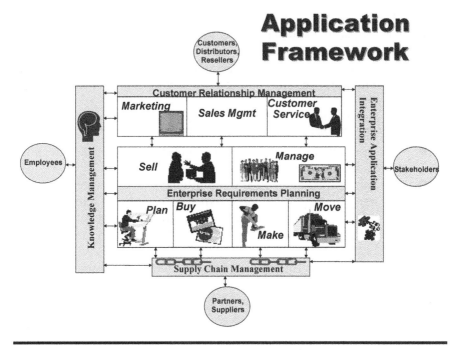

Figure 7.3   High Level Application Framework

on high value customers, bidirectional communication, and proactive opportunity management. Marketing must develop a proactive strategy to get customers to the Web site. Advertising, promotions, marketing campaigns, and materials are created, implemented, and monitored electronically. Literature is distributed electronically. Customer-specific preferences as well as profiling and personalization capabilities are tracked. A virtual storefront is provided with an electronic product catalog and catalog personalization. Customer predictive modeling is done to analyze customer behavior and preferences, click stream analysis, demographic analysis, and target audience identification. Event scheduling and tracking are done online. Pricing, contracts, and price analysis are done electronically.

■ **E-Sales Management:** E-sales management optimizes the efficiency and effectiveness of a company's direct sales force through Internet-enabled communication and systems integration. The sales force is fully automated and coordinated with integrated information. Leads and contacts are generated, tracked, and managed electronically. Sales prospects and customer contacts are managed online with calendar, time management, and task lists. Quotes and proposals are created

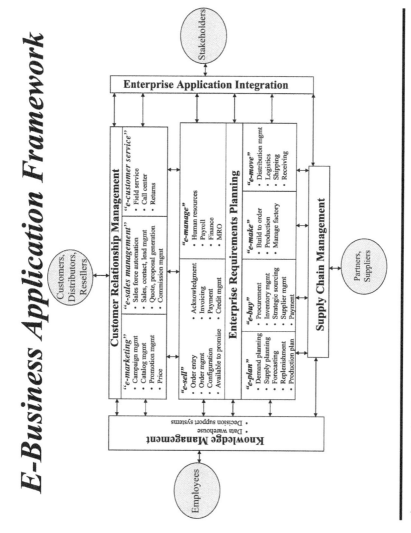

Figure 7.4 Application Framework

and distributed electronically. Commissions are calculated and distributed electronically. Sales effectiveness is tracked and monitored online with pipeline analysis, sales metrics, and territory alignment. The telemarketing program support is electronic for both inbound and outbound calls with call list assembly, auto dialing, scripting, and call tracking.

■ **E-Customer Service:** E-customer service increases the company's ability to respond to customer inquiries, complaints, and requests with higher efficiency and effectiveness. The call center is managed electronically and integrated with the PBX telephony. The majority of calls are resolved through Internet self-service functionality, frequently asked questions, and online chat. Customer complaints are handled, problem resolution is tracked, and corrective action reporting is done. Customer service includes incident assignment, escalation, tracking, and reporting as well as problem management and warranty management. Service-level agreements are managed electronically. E-marketing, e-sales, and e-customer service are often combined into Customer Relationship Management (CRM) systems. Examples of CRM systems include Clarify, Siebel, Vantive, Pivotal, SalesLogix, and Saratoga.

■ **E-Sell:** E-sell enables companies to sell their products and services over the Internet. Relationships with customers are streamlined with real-time connections and information, including self-service order entry, with product configuration, pricing (including contracts and discounts), and credit authorization. Real-time consultative selling and online knowledge-based sales assistance are provided. Product substitution advice is provided as well as up-selling and cross-selling prompting. Product availability and real-time available-to-promise capability are ensured. Invoices and payments are processed electronically. Real-time order status information and e-mail notifications are provided.

■ **E-Manage:** E-manage improves the effectiveness and efficiency of managing the overall organization. Employee training and communication are handled electronically. Real-time employee profiles are viewed and updated by employees. Payroll functions and funds are transferred electronically. Expenses are recorded and approved. Funds are transferred electronically. Financial information is available real-time so the books can close minutes after the last transaction. Maintenance, repair, and operating supplies (MRO) are managed, controlled, and processed electronically.

■ **E-Plan:** E-plan organizes the demand and supply collaboratively throughout the value chain. This includes collaborative design, planning, forecasting, and replenishment. The focus is on constrained components and collecting true demand. E-plan includes vendor-managed inventory, production schedule optimization, advanced planning and scheduling, and inventory management. Demand and supply planning and scheduling examples are i2 and Manugistics.

■ **E-Buy:** E-buy streamlines relationships with suppliers by utilizing the Internet to provide real-time connections and information. Inventory is replaced with information. Electronic catalogs provide all information on materials and services. Strategic sourcing is supported worldwide. E-buy handles the purchase requisition, obtains authorization and approvals electronically, converts the requisition to a purchase order, and communicates the order to an approved supplier. Electronic acknowledgement of receipt of goods or services and electronic payment to the supplier are made. Supplier performance is electronic and real-time.

■ **E-Make:** E-make synchronizes the execution of build-to-order production activities. Lean manufacturing techniques are employed. Exception signals are automated and problems are corrected quickly. The production floor is managed electronically.

■ **E-Move:** E-move optimizes the efficiency and effectiveness of shipping, distribution, warehouse management, receiving, and transportation management. Shipping option alternatives are provided online. Manifesting, documentation, and carrier information are electronic and integrated. Virtual warehousing is supported.

■ **Supply Chain Management:** Supply chain management is the collaborative electronic integration of information and processes with a web of value partners. Demand and capacity is understood, and capacity is scheduled to meet demand. Real-time, global, available-to-promise capability is provided through the entire value chain.

■ **Knowledge Management:** Knowledge management provides online, real-time information to manage the business and support business decisions. Volumes of data are transformed into meaningful information and knowledge. Data marts are provided with multiple and flexible views to support the dynamic business. A real-time balanced scorecard is provided for all management, which connects the business strategy with investments, continuous improvement, and daily decision making. It provides insight into the critical performance factors for the business. Data mining utilizes analytical tools with artificial intelligence to uncover patterns and relationships in large amounts of data. Knowledge management also provides tools to understand, classify, or summarize text. Examples of knowledge management tools include Hyperion, Cognos, Business Objects, and Oracle.

■ **Enterprise Application Integration:** Enterprise application integration synchronizes front-office, back-office, and supply chain activities. It provides much needed systems integration, which is a requirement for corporate agility.

Now draft the business application requirements section of your e-business plan document. Identify the key business application areas and functions for your company. Discuss which areas of business applications are critical to e-enable and why. Identify any weak areas of business applications that hinder integration and Internet progress due to the age, technical structure, or current functionality of the application.

TECHNICAL ARCHITECTURE IMPACT

E-business has definitely put more emphasis, requirements, and stress on the technical architecture than ever before. As shown in Figure 7.5, there are also more components in the technical architecture than there have been in the past. Architectures are typically n-tier, meaning that any number of servers may be involved in a transaction. Opening up the technical infrastructure to the world adds new complexities and challenges that were not as great in the past. System reliability, availability, performance, scalability, flexibility, and security are critical to the success of a business. The penalty for systems failures is greater than ever, resulting in lost customers, falling stock prices, bad publicity, or even government action. To meet these requirements, there are many new devices, techniques, and designs available. There are more options and choices available than there ever have been in the past. One way to help make it through this continuously changing sea of options is to make sure that the technical architecture is driven by the business strategy and to make technical decisions as part of an overall e-business planning process.

The architecture should be planned and designed to handle and balance the e-business requirements, as shown in Figure 7.6:

- **Availability and reliability:** The e-business architecture must be designed so that no single point of failure exists. Replication and redundancy are ways to address availability and reliability. Replication copies data to an alternate copy of the database. One decision on replication is the frequency, if it is worth the expense to do it every 5 minutes vs. every 8 hours. Redundancy has live backups, including redundant servers, server farms, and communication links. Design network bandwidth and server capacity to handle many times the average load because e-business volumes can be very unpredictable. Examples of designs include storing copies of content on different servers and ISPs across the world or routing traffic to servers with the least amount of load. For example, www.barnsandnoble.com uses multiple server farms with a cluster of servers in New York and replicated servers at hosting facilities operated by America Online

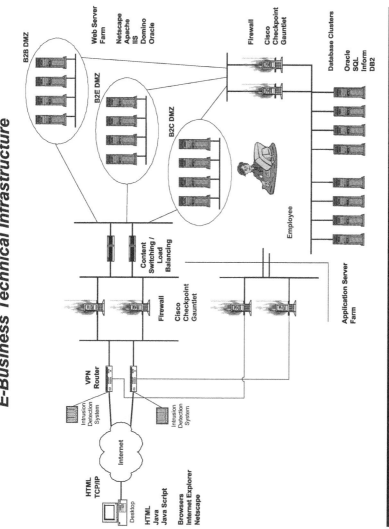

Figure 7.5 E-Business Technical Architecture

Balancing E-Business Requirements

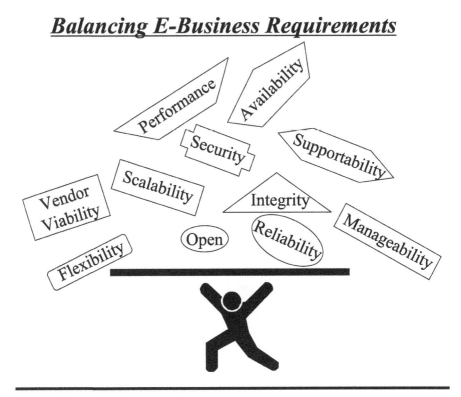

Figure 7.6   Balancing E-Business Requirements

and Cable & Wireless PLC. They use Cisco Systems' Distributed Director for load-balancing to direct traffic to servers that can best process the transactions. Other load-balancing products work locally to route to servers within a server farm (examples include Big/ip appliance from F5 Inc, Ipivot Inc.). If load-balancing or clustering is implemented be sure to provide high availability so that there is enough capacity if one of the components in the firewall cluster is lost. Otherwise, an outage or service impact could occur even with clustering.

■ **Scalability and performance:** A system is scalable when performance can increase or decrease in increments with little or no disruption. This flexibility is required to handle sudden increases and decreases in volume due to business changes such as mergers, acquisitions, divestitures, new marketing promotions, new products, or new customers. Forecasting the traffic that a new service or business change will attract is difficult, so systems must be flexible to quickly accommodate changes in volume. As architectures today are complex and have many components, many different factors could cause performance issues. There are many tactics and options available to assist with scalability and performance issues, including:

— The traditional solution has been to add more bandwidth and processors to improve performance and transport more traffic. If a 56-Kbps line is overloaded, upgrade to a T1 (1.5-Mbps); if that fills up add more or go to fractional or full T3 (up to 45-Mbps). Additional firewalls, network switches, or server capacity can always be added. This option can be expensive and may not solve all the problems.

— Use multiple servers and clusters to process transactions with load balancing techniques. Load balancing can be done at the server level as well as the switch communications level. Clustering groups of independent servers to work as a single system will improve overall performance.

— Offload encryption transactions to another server as encrypted transactions can impact performance (e.g., Commerce Accelerator from Ipivot).

— Outsource to an ISP to build and manage to documented service levels (e.g., DBN, Digex, Digital Island, Exodus Communications, Frontier Communications, Level 3, Qwest, Usinternetworking).

— Put frequently accessed information closer to the users, particularly for bandwidth-intensive content. Distribute services in different geographical areas. Distribute or replicate data such as graphics and large files to servers closer to customers. Use graphics or database caching, which stores seldom updated content. This pushes the content further down the network so it does not have to travel through as many switches or servers.

— Rewrite program code for optimization. Use stored procedures when possible. To make applications perform at peak, developers can invest time in optimization for a specific environment and conditions.

— Tune servers through thread pooling and other techniques. Each server must be optimized individually, and the tiers or farms of servers must also be optimized as a group.

— Policy-based networking can prioritize certain customer traffic over others. It can give certain customers or workgroups priority or assign bandwidth to specific e-business services. An example of this software is Alteon Inc.

— Performance measurement and monitoring services are available from companies such as Keynote Systems Inc. and Net.Genesis Inc.

■ **Security and integrity:** Security has been a concern since the beginning of the Internet. When designing for security, assume the worst and design strong protection with multiple layers. Consider security risks from external entities as well as internal authorized users either with malicious intent or unintentionally. Transaction integrity must be considered in the design. Directory-level security, encryption, and digital certificates are options to consider. Are enough firewalls utilized, and are they in the right locations? Does the organization have a hot-standby solution? Has the organization considered encryption/decryption in the hardware?

■ **Flexible and open:** Flexibility is critical for success, to meet changing business and technical requirements. An architecture is flexible if it is easy to make changes to processes, applications, or technology. The technical architecture needs to be flexible enough to facilitate interactions from the customer through PCs, PDAs, phones, and other devices and methods. The systems must be flexible to support the complexity of integrating business-to-business transactions as well as business-to-consumer transactions.

■ **Manageability and supportability:** The systems must be able to provide consistent service quality with low administration and overhead. In a highly dynamic e-business environment, loads and volumes shift dramatically and quickly. Tools and management systems must be able to adapt quickly and keep the critical e-business transactions processing smoothly. There are real-time end-to-end performance management tools available for proactive or immediate notification of faults and problems throughout the e-business infrastructure. Alarms can be sent when a defined threshold is reached. There are also trend-based or historical performance management tools available that collect data and present a picture of how the infrastructure is performing. IBM's Tivoli, Computer Associates' Universe, and HP OpenView are examples of tools that are available.

■ **Vendor viability:** With all the fast-moving changes in technology and business startups, mergers, acquisitions, and failures, it is a chall-enge to select vendor-supplied software and hardware that will be able to withstand the test of time and be in existence in a few years.

The following questions should be asked regarding the technical architecture:

■ What technical infrastructure must be in place to support the e-business requirements?
■ What are the speed, stability, and availability requirements?

- What are the service-level requirements?
- What are the network bandwidth requirements?
- What are the computing resource requirements?
- Is there sufficient hardware (firewalls, network switches, servers, network lines) in place for the potential traffic? Have bandwidth and server capacity been estimated at many times the average load?
- Are there any single points of failure in the architecture?
- Has replication been considered? How often will replication take place and what is the cost?
- Has mirroring been considered to keep copies dynamically up to date?
- Is the architecture scalable?
- Have redundancy, load balancing, and clustering been considered? Can the capacity in a cluster handle the additional load if a component goes down?
- Have caching and distribution of data and graphics been considered?
- Has a network policy been developed with priorities identified?
- Are there both real-time and historical performance measurement and monitoring tools available? Are they used consistently? Who reviews the data? How frequently? What action is taken?
- Is security sufficient?
- Who gets access? When do they get access? How do they get access?
- Is security administration distributed or centralized?
- How is self-administration minimized while still keeping the environment secure?
- How is management alerted to security breaches or issues?
- How is loss or corruption of data prevented during transmission?
- Have software and hardware components been selected from reputable, solid, and secure vendors?
- What support levels are provided by each vendor?

The e-business requirements on the technical architecture are definitely a challenge to meet as shown by Figure 7.7. With all these requirements, it is also important to manage both investment and risk.

To meet these challenges, an associate goes by the mantra "Simplify, standardize, integrate, and automate," as shown in Figure 7.8. This strategy will definitely drive the technical architecture closer to an e-enabled organization:

- **Simplify:** Whenever possible or reasonable, eliminate redundant components. Select products that are simple to install, administer, and support. Consider long-term cost of ownership before purchasing new components. Minimize the number of differing infrastructure components.

Managing a complex environment is difficult and expensive.

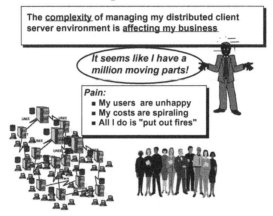

Figure 7.7 Managing a Complex Environment

A solid foundation is required to deliver e-business

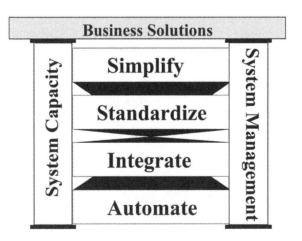

Figure 7.8 Simplify, Standardize, Integrate, and Automate

■ **Standardize:** Clearly defined standards will direct subsequent architecture choices. Without standards, it is very difficult (or impossible) to become an e-enabled enterprise. With standards, it is easier, cheaper, and faster to deploy new applications and functionality. A standards-based architecture increases the ability to adapt to changes. Duplication is minimized, and the architecture is more scalable. It is less expensive because components can be reused. Standardize with vendor-supplied packages whenever possible rather than developing software in house. This will lower the risk, allow quicker implementation, and save money. Reduce the number of technologies and platforms that are deployed. Minimize the number of different vendors rather than choosing best of breed.

■ **Integrate:** Integrate both internally and externally to customers, suppliers, partners, and employees. Components of the architecture should integrate so well that bridges and special code do not have to be maintained for the components to work together. Systems should function together transparently.

■ **Automate:** Management of the architecture should be automated whenever possible. This is accomplished through event management facilities and other functions. If new hardware is necessary to support e-business, care must be taken to ensure the new hardware fits well within the existing infrastructure and meets all the business and technical requirements. Exhibit 7.1 shows examples of questions to ask when purchasing or considering new hardware, whether servers, disk, switches, or others.

Now draft the technical infrastructure section of your e-business plan document. Ensure the new infrastructure meets the new e-business requirements.

BUSINESS PROCESS IMPACT

The single largest, and often overlooked, challenge to e-enabling an enterprise is redesigning business processes. Many times in an organization, business processes have just evolved as the company has grown. The processes may not have evolved into the most efficient and effective processes. Even if processes have been redesigned in the recent past, technology may now enable even more improvements. Organizational barriers inside or outside the organization may also have hindered improvements in the past. The entire information flow within a value chain should be redesigned and considered. Sometimes, the greatest opportunities can be improving flow between companies. Individual company processes may have, at times, suboptimized the processes within an entire value chain. Well-defined and seamless business processes are a requirement for an efficient e-enabled organization and value chain.

Exhibit 7.1 Hardware Acquisition Questions

■ **Stability:**
 — How reliably does it deliver the services for which it is intended?
 — How does the stability (actual vs. planed availability) statistics of hardware compare to its competitors?

■ **Features:**
 — How well does the feature set compare to the alternatives?
 — How does the product rate on published product feature comparisons?

■ **Performance:**
 — How is performance on the component measured? (transactions per second, time to open a file, duration of batch job)
 — How does the product rate on published performance statistics?

■ **Manageability:**
 — To what extent can the platform provide management tools or be managed through commercial management tools?
 — How are performance monitoring and tuning, fault detection and automated fault handling, configuration and change management handled in the product?

■ **Compatibility:**
 — Does the hardware work with existing components, releases, and operating systems?
 — Does a vendor that you currently have offer the product to reduce the number of vendors involved?

■ **Value:**
 — Does the company get some new characteristics or the same characteristics for less money?

■ **Maturity:**
 — What is the product's position in the expected life cycle?
 — Is the product innovative, leading edge, accepted, commodity, or obsolete?

■ **Market Position:**
 — What is the product's market share?
 — Is the vendor a technology leader, dominator, major player, entrant, niche player, fringe player, or orphan?
 — What are the public's thoughts regarding the product's future market share?

■ **Vendor Stability:**
 — How long has the vendor been in business?
 — What is the financial health of the vendor?
 — Is the market unstable with many acquisitions?
 — What are the public's thoughts regarding the vendor's future market share?
 — Is the vendor responsive and easy to work with?

Exhibit 7.1   Hardware Acquisition Questions (continued)

■ **Cost of Ownership:**
  — What is the overall cost of ownership of the hardware?
  — How does it compare to the existing hardware?
  — What is the projected residual value?
  — Is maintenance support necessary?

■ **Implementation:**
  — What are the implementation considerations?
  — What training will be necessary, what procedures must be updated, space considerations, UPS and electrical considerations?
  — What are the testing requirements? What interfaces should be tested? What conversions are necessary? What metrics should be monitored after implementation?
  — If it is replacing existing hardware, is there any residual value of old hardware? Is there any cost to dispose of old hardware?
  — What impact will it have on the disaster recovery plan?

■ **Maintenance and Support:**
  — What are the various support plans? Is support available 24 hours a day, 7 days a week?
  — What is the cost of the various support plans?
  — Do you get acceptable response when trying the hot-line?
  — Can troubleshooting be done remotely?

■ **Purchase Considerations:**
  — What is better for your situation, lease or purchase?
  — What is the discount percent? Can the company obtain volume purchases if other hardware is owned or purchased from the vendor?
  — What are the terms and conditions?
  — What are the payment terms?
  — What additional charges or implementation costs are there?
  — What is the availability of hardware? Is it back-ordered?
  — What would be the scheduled delivery and install date?
  — Are there any options to order or consider?

E-business is an enabling technology, but the true value cannot be realized until business processes are redesigned and new ways of working are adopted. Wal-Mart is an example of an organization that has been a proactive leader in its industry to drive new processes throughout its value chain.

There are many potential benefits to redesigning processes across the entire supply chain as shown in Figure 7.9:

  ■ Reduce overhead costs
  ■ Decrease time to market

Benefits of Redesigning Supply Chain Processes

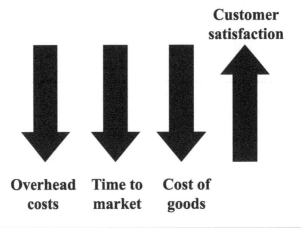

Figure 7.9   Benefits of Redesigning Supply Chain Processes

- Decrease cost of goods
- Increase customer satisfaction

Some questions to help guide the overall process improvement effort include:

- What business processes need to change to handle the e-business customer expectations?
- How can business processes be integrated throughout the value chain?
- Are the business processes automated?
- Are the business processes and information fully integrated?
- Do the processes cross throughout the organization?
- Does each process have metrics to measure the effectiveness and efficiency of the process?
- How does the organization know if processes are broken or need improvement?
- Is there a culture of continuous improvement?
- Are processes designed to do the right work and to do the work right the first time? Are processes designed to prevent errors?
- How can best practices of the various business units be combined?
- Do processes have corrective action designed so that the root cause is determined and fixed?
- Are processes documented and followed consistently?

- How can the processes be streamlined from the outside in, from the customer's perspective? Look at product configuration, manufacturing, shipment and delivery, presales and postsales service, billing, and credit-checking.
- Are orders processed quickly enough?
- Can items be ordered from multiple divisions?
- How can the direct customer interfacing processes be streamlined?
- How do the product and order process look from a customer standpoint?
- Is customer satisfaction measured and acted upon on a regular basis?
- Is the customer profile company-wide? Who ensures its accuracy?
- How will leads be pursued and turned into sales?
- How quickly will questions and requests be handled?
- How will information provided on registrations be utilized?
- How will Internet sales be compensated?
- What process will be utilized to update content on the Web site?
- How will employees be kept aware of changing content?

Ask the following questions about each process:

- Is the process defined, documented, and understood by all process participants?
- Does the process have an owner who is responsible for its performance?
- Can the process be measured?
- Are metrics from the process reviewed on a regular basis and appropriate action taken?
- Is user satisfaction measured for the process on a regular basis by asking those who receive output from the process?
- Is the process automated with tools?
- Is the process optimized to reduce unnecessary interventions and wait times?
- Is each activity in the process necessary?
- Is the process improved on a regular basis?
- Are roles and responsibilities documented?
- Does the process cross the organization or the supply chain? Has it been optimized?

Challenge the basics of the business processes by thinking outside the box. For example, rather than asking how to improve the credit-checking process, ask if the credit-checking process is necessary at all. Rather than asking how to reduce inventory, ask why inventory is needed at all. Start with a blank sheet of paper. The largest value can be derived from the largest changes. Be sure to uncover opportunities that can be found between process steps. Don't confine the review to processes within departments. Look at processes that cross the organization and processes that go outside the organization for redesign efforts that will have the greatest impact.

Now draft the business process section of your e-business plan document.

IS PROCESS IMPACT

Just as the business processes must be redesigned, so must the information systems processes. This area is also often overlooked until there are problems, such as:

■ The e-business system crashes due to a change that was recently implemented, and the organization realizes the change control process is not rigorous enough.

■ The e-mail system crashes due to capacity issues and the organization realizes that the capacity and storage management process is not as active as it should be.

■ The supply chain management system is down longer than it should be due to issues in the problem management process.

■ A new e-business application has serious issues that were not found in testing due to inadequacies in the testing process.

■ A new Internet application was rushed to market and implemented. It did not meet the business requirements because the systems development methodology was not followed for that application.

The list of potential issues could go on and on. With information systems directly in front of the public and customers, any information systems issues are immediately obvious. These issues that we used to be disappointed with, but tolerated in the past, can now impact stock prices, generate company publicity, and result in embarrassment, legal action, or lost customers. The only way to improve the quality and consistency of information systems is to improve the information systems processes.

Figure 7.10 identifies typical processes found in an information systems organization. This chart is from my previous book, *A Practical Guide to Information Systems Process Improvement* (CRC Press, 2000), which outlines a step-by-step methodology for improving information systems processes. In addition to the process questions listed in the business process section, the following questions will help evaluate information systems processes:

■ How do the information systems processes need to change to support the e-business requirements?

■ Are capacity and storage managed properly to meet the volatile e-business needs?

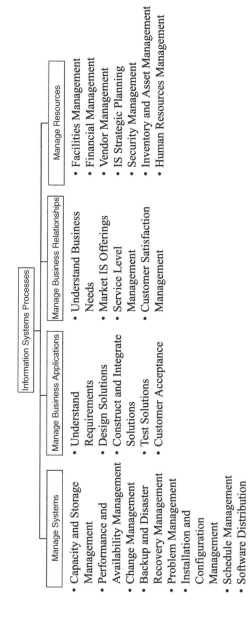

Figure 7.10   Information Systems Processes

- What are the service-level requirements? Is the organization meeting them?
- Is change control complete enough? Have changes been implemented with no impact?
- Are systems and data backed up on a regular basis? Does a disaster recovery plan exist? Has it been tested?
- What is the mean time to fix issues? Is the problem management quick enough to handle e-business issues with minimal impact?
- Are hardware and software documented and upgrades planned without issue?
- Are jobs documented and run successfully and uneventfully?
- Is software distribution managed and executed properly?
- Are systems developed and projects completed on time and within budget? Do they meet the required functionality?
- Is the Information Systems organization integrated seamlessly with the business? Are internal customers satisfied with the support and communication from Information Systems?
- Are facilities managed to minimize risk and issues?
- Are finances controlled and managed to provide a positive return?
- Are vendors managed properly to minimize cost and optimize the value chain?
- Does Information Systems have a direction that is aligned with the business direction?
- Is security managed to minimize risk and disruption to the business?
- Are assets managed to obtain the lowest total cost of ownership?
- Are key business and technical statistics gathered, reported, and managed?
- Are owners of services well defined?
- Are processes regularly improved?
- Are employees satisfied?

Now draft the information systems process section of your e-business plan document.

PEOPLE/ORGANIZATION IMPACT

As e-business impacts the processes in an organization, it can also impact the organization structures, culture, job responsibilities, and titles of individuals. Changes impacting people must be carefully implemented with attention to change management. Many times, new processes and technology fail because the organization fails to recognize and manage the human components of the change. The following are suggestions for managing these changes:

- Communicate, communicate, and then communicate some more. Communication must be continuous, clear, complete, enthusiastic, simple, and honest. Incomplete information will often be filled in by rumor. Communicate clearly the strategy, goals, and objectives that require the changes. Communicate as honestly as possible the personal impact the changes will have on each individual.
- Identify the magnitude of the change. What areas and people are most impacted? How can this change be managed?
- Define and document new roles and responsibilities.
- Ensure the structure supports the new processes and goals. Make sure proper resources exist to support the new processes.
- Ask individuals to help implement the change. Obtain commitment and involvement.
- Visibly and actively provide leadership.
- Train individuals to support their new responsibilities and the new technology. Do not underestimate the training required to support changes.
- Identify and communicate the metrics to measure performance.
- Make sure that incentives match the new goals and processes. Recognize and reward those who help make the change.
- Listen to feedback and adjust if necessary.

The following questions will provide assistance with the people and organizational changes:

- What is the required skill set for developing and implementing the e-business systems?
- What is the required skill set to support the e-business systems?
- Does the organization have the necessary skill set and resources that can be allocated to developing and implementing the e-business systems?
- Who in the business is responsible for content development and updating? Is it recognized as part of the individual's job?
- How will e-business impact the sales force?
- Who will respond to questions that are submitted on the Web site?
- Who will respond to literature requests?
- Who will compile information provided on registrations?
- Who will update customer lists?
- Who will monitor and improve customer satisfaction?
- What orientation and training is required?
- Are there sufficient resources assigned?
- Are new or changed responsibilities defined and documented?

- Is there appropriate backup of responsibilities and knowledge for the business areas?
- How will the performance of individuals be measured? How about the performance of the group?
- What incentives are needed to encourage and promote e-solutions in the organization? Do incentives match the goals?
- Are cross-functional teams in place to improve e-business processes?

Outsourcing is often discussed as a potential solution for the question if the organization has the necessary skill set and can allocate those resources for the development and implementation of an e-business solution. In addition to having the proper skill set, the issue is often one of speed to market, and the need to support maintenance or other critical company initiatives and projects. The following are factors to consider in deciding if the organization should complete the development with internal resources or partner with external resources:

- Does the organization have the skill set in Internet development tools?
- How much experience does the organization have in Internet design, development, and implementation?
- Does the organization have fresh, out-of-the-box, up-to-date thinking?
- Can the organization allocate these resources to the e-business effort?
- Can the organization deliver the functionality in the necessary timeframe?

A company may require additional assistance. Exhibit 7.2 shows examples of questions to assist in selection of a Web development company according to the categories illustrated in Figure 7.11.

In addition to external development resources, a company may choose to outsource the operation of e-business through a service provider. There are several different types of outsourcing or service providers:

- **ISP:** Internet service provider, providing the hardware and software for your Internet site.
- **ASP:** Application service provider, supplying application rentals where the organization can pay by the hour to use business applications or the data center. Examples of vendors include Corio, Interliant, Qwest Cyber.Solutions, and Usinternetworking.
- **VSP:** Vertical service providers, offering expertise in the industry, such as financial or health care.
- **SSP:** Security service providers, offering additional security protection services.

Exhibit 7.2   Web Development Company Questions

Experience:
■ Specifically what Web sites has the company developed? Look at the Web sites to see if you like the designs.
  — Are the designs unique?
  — Are the sites efficient and loaded quickly?
  — Are the sites easy to navigate and understand?
  — Were the customers satisfied?
  — What impact did the e-business functionality have on their businesses?
■ How long has the company been designing and developing Web sites?
■ How many Web sites has it developed?
■ Has it developed sites in your specific industry?
■ What tools and software is the company experienced with?

Resources:
■ Specifically what resources will be assigned to the effort?
■ Are the resources knowledgeable, experienced, and easy to work with?

Approach:
■ How does the vendor manage its projects?
■ Does the vendor develop and maintain a project plan and provide periodic updates?

Company:
■ How long has the vendor been in business?
■ What is the financial health of the vendor?
■ Is the market unstable with many acquisitions?
■ What are the public's thoughts regarding the vendor's future market share?
■ Is the vendor responsive and easy to work with?

Cost:
■ What is the estimated cost?
■ Is the cost fixed or variable?
■ What factors could result in a cost increase or decrease?
■ Is there a penalty for late delivery?
■ Is there a bonus for early delivery?

■ **WASP:** Wireless application service provider, supplying wireless applications and services to businesses.
■ **MSP:** Management service providers manage applications, networks, systems, storage, and security. They provide performance monitoring. Examples of vendors include Nuclio, Silverback Technologies, SiteRock, Totality, and Triactive.
■ **SSP:** Storage service providers provide hosting and access to storage devices. Examples of vendors include Comdisco, Compaq Global Services, IBM Global Services, StorageNetworks, and Storability.

Selecting a Web Development Company

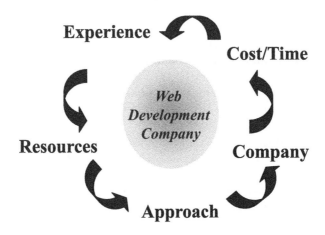

Figure 7.11   Selecting a Web Development Company

- **BCSP:** Business continuity service providers define and document procedures for assessing, responding to, and recovering from disasters. Examples of vendors include Comdisco, Compaq Global Services, EDS, IBM Global Services, and SiteSmith.
- **CSP:** HelpDesk/Customer service providers handle e-mail and calls. Examples of vendors include CompuCom Systems, IHS Helpdesk Service, Service Management International, and Stream International.

Although outsourcing to a service provider may cost the organization more over the long term, it saves the initial cost in developing an infrastructure if the organization's infrastructure is lacking. Outsourcing can also reduce the amount of time to implement a new environment. However, be careful as you select service providers, because the organization will be handing over mission critical data and functions to an outsider. The selection of a service provider is critical for the success of e-business in the organization.

The following Web sites have excellent service provider information:

- www.thelist.com
- www.isp-planet.com
- www.cnet.com

Consider the following facts:

- Sites that are down cost an average of $8,000 per hour in lost revenue (Forrester).

Service Provider Requirements

- Service level agreements
- Availability, reliability
- Scalability, growth
- Performance
- Security
- Disaster recovery
- Access
- Reporting
- Technical support

- Environment
- Processes, procedures
- People
- Company
- References
- Partnership
- Price
- Implementation
- Termination

Figure 7.12   Service Provider Requirements

■ For dot coms, the sites are their brands. A total of 47% of users experiencing technical difficulty while downloading a page on a first visit abandon the site. Approximately 9% of those visitors never return (Jupiter).

■ The average web browser waits 8 seconds for a web page download, where the average is about 10 seconds (Zona Research). The difference accounts for $4.35B in lost e-commerce sales.

The selection of a service provider is critical to the organization's e-business success. An organization that does not ask the right questions up front could pay the price later. Hiring the wrong service provider can spell death to a company. Make a checklist of the requirements and spend the time to investigate the service providers thoroughly. Obtain and review documentation. Talk to current and past customers. Asking the right questions is critical to finding an affordable and reliable service provider. As shown in Figure 7.12, there are typically many requirements for a service provider. Exhibit 7.3 shows sample questions to ask a service provider.

Now draft the people/organization section of your e-business plan document.

COST/BENEFIT ANALYSIS

Although it may be difficult to estimate the costs of e-business ventures, it is important that the organization goes into an e-business venture with an idea of the level of investment that will be required. It is important to include all the costs so the organization is not surprised part way down the path and unable to continue the efforts. Ask the following questions:

Exhibit 7.3 Service Provider Questions

Service level agreements:

■ What are the service provider's typical metrics for service level?

■ What are the service-level objectives? What is the minimum amount of service level that will be stipulated in the contract?

■ How often has the service provider met or not met the service level objectives? What has been the history of compliance?

■ What are the methods and process for reporting service levels?

■ How does the service provider ensure customer satisfaction?

■ How can the metrics be audited?

■ What are the specific components of each metric?

■ What are the penalties for not meeting service level agreements?

■ Does the service provider give prorated refunds for downtime?

Availability and reliability:

■ Are there any single points of failure in the technical architecture?

■ What measures are taken for replication?

■ What measures are taken for redundancy (repetition)?

■ What measures are taken for diversity (physical independence)?

■ Examples to consider: load balancing, clustering, access router, customer router, local access, backbone nodes, interoffice channel, POP.

■ What tools are used for proactive notification of issues?

■ What is their up time?

■ Do they have hot spares available on site?

Scalable, growth capacity:

■ What is the process and how long does it take to implement new hardware to handle increased loads?

■ What are the smallest and largest sizes and volumes that the service provider will handle?

■ Can the service provider meet the organization's growth plans?

■ What are the service provider's growth plans?

■ Can the organization have unlimited bandwidth or visitor counts?

■ Can the organization have unlimited FTP access?

■ Can the organization have unlimited storage?

■ Can encryption transactions be off-loaded?

■ What forecasting and modeling tools are used?

Performance:

■ Review logs of performance statistics: What are the number of outages, length of outages, busy and capacity statistics?

■ What is the service provider's bandwidth utilization?

■ What does the service provider consider peak loads?

■ Review run book and operations documentation.

■ Does the service provider do automatic load balancing?

Exhibit 7.3   Service Provider Questions (continued)

■ Does the service provider provide a content distribution architecture?
■ What is the service provider's process for reviewing performance and tuning servers and other hardware?
■ What performance measurement and monitoring tools are used?
■ Does the service provider warranty or guarantee bandwidth throughput?

Security:
■ How often is data backed up?
■ How often are backups stored off site?
■ Are security policies and procedures documented? Review the documentation.
■ Review documented responses to security incidents.
■ What intrusion prevention measures and tracking are used?
■ What intrusion tests and annual security audits are completed?
■ Is physical access controlled and access logged?
■ Is there a confidentiality agreement that is signed?
■ What accountability is there for theft or damage of data?
■ What are the specific security administration responsibilities?
■ What audit trails are performed?
■ What firewalls, authentication, and encryption systems are used?
■ How serious is the general awareness of security?
■ Is client data isolated with sensitive data encrypted end to end?
■ Is the security program built upon accepted standards, such as British Standard 7799?

Disaster recovery:
■ Review the disaster recovery plan and process.
■ How long is the backup battery power?
■ How long is the backup generator?
■ What are power, cooling, and fire prevention standards?
■ Is a hot site provided?

Access:
■ What access is provided, private line, Frame, ATM?
■ Are speeds from 56 Kbps to 622 Mbps (OC12)?
■ What locations are supported?
■ Is there a limit of access hours per month?
■ What time and days will the system be unavailable because of scheduled outages and maintenance?

Reporting:
■ How is usage reported?
■ How is customer information reported?
■ Review the reports that are provided on a weekly and monthly basis.

Exhibit 7.3 Service Provider Questions (continued)

Technical support:
- Is support provided 24 hours a day, 7 days a week?
- Is support provided via phone (toll free) and e-mail?
- Review statistics on the support desk (average length of time to resolve issue, length of time to answer call, length of time on hold, etc.).
- Is there a direct dial number for emergencies?
- Where does the service provider's responsibility end and the company's responsibility begin?

Hardware environment:
- What spare parts and equipment are carried on site?
- What is the average time to make repairs?
- What is the age of equipment and preventive maintenance schedule?

Software environment:
- What file types are supported?
- How are software licenses controlled?
- What responsibilities are there relative to software licenses?

Processes and procedures:
- Review the documentation.
- How much flexibility is available?
- Does the service provider have the ability to tailor response to problems and events?
- Is the change management process documented?
- What is the process for monitoring vendor and third-party bug lists and applying patches and updates?
- How often is maintenance scheduled?
- Is the service provider current on software and hardware releases?
- When will maintenance impact availability?

People:
- What is the defined staffing level?
- What capabilities and certifications do personnel have?
- How does the service provider hire, train, and retain employees?
- Does the service provider conduct criminal background checks and drug tests?
- What is the turnover rate?
- What level of expertise will be on the account?
- Who will be the specific customer advocate?
- Who will be the specific technical liaison?

Vendor company viability and stability:
- What many active customers does the service provider currently have?
- How many customers have switched away from the service provider? Why did they leave?
- Who is the service provider's largest customer?

Exhibit 7.3   Service Provider Questions (continued)

- What is the average length of time customers have been with the service provider?
- How many years has the service provider been in business (should be in business at least 4 years)?
- What local and regional presence does the service provider have?
- Does the service provider have a good and informative Web site?
- What is the financial status and viability of the service provider?
- What is the growth rate of the service provider?
- What is the future direction of the service provider?
- What planned enhancements does the service provider have?
- What enhancements has the service provider made in the past year?

Customer references:

- What references does the service provider have with situations similar to yours and which have been with the service provider a minimum of 1 year?
- Call at least three other customers and talk to them at length.
- Check www.isp.com for reviews from users in your area.

Partnership:

- Does the service provider have a willingness to work with the company?
- Do the company culture and values of the service provider match your company? Is it a good fit?

Price:

- Is the price a flat rate or burstable (usage-based) billing?
- What is the discount structure?
- Is there a discount for multiyear contracts?
- Is there a minimal set-up cost?
- Is there a free trial period?
- Are the subscription plan options understandable?
- Are there prepayments?
- Is the connection a local call with the telephone company?
- Are there surcharges for 800 dial-up connections?

Implementation:

- What support is provided during the transition?
- What are the specific responsibilities of both parties?
- What guarantees are provided?
- What testing and parallel services are provided prior to implementation?
- What additional options and services are offered for implementation or on an ongoing basis?

Termination:

- What are the termination clauses and requirements?
- What is the commitment term?
- What are the responsibilities of both parties in termination?
- Does the service provider provide assistance with switching providers?

Exhibit 7.3   Service Provider Questions (continued)

■ Can the business obtain regular deliveries of backup tapes?
■ What is the definition of property if the agreement is terminated, including domain names, software, and data?
■ What is the service guarantee?
■ What is the definition of customer satisfaction? How is it measured?
■ Are there penalties for early termination?
■ Is there a specified grace period?

relative to costs:

■ How much will hardware cost for the necessary infrastructure improvements?
■ Are there any service provider costs?
■ How much will software cost for the necessary infrastructure improvements?
■ How much will internal and external labor cost to make the necessary infrastructure improvements?
■ How much will the software cost for the necessary business application improvements?
■ How much will internal and external labor cost for the business application improvements?
■ How much will training cost to support the business applications as well as process changes that are necessary? How much travel cost is required for the training?
■ How much will it cost for re-engineering the business processes?
■ How much will the interfaces to other applications or organizations cost?
■ How much will the conversions cost?
■ What are the opportunity costs? What will not get completed as a result of focusing resources on e-business?
■ What are the total costs?
■ What are the one-time costs?
■ What are the recurring costs?
■ How much should the organization expect to allocate to keeping e-business abreast of market and customer changes on an ongoing basis?
■ What are the unquantifiable or qualitative costs that will be incurred?

Estimating e-business costs is a challenge, but estimating the benefits of e-business is even more of a challenge. Companies have control over the costs, but have considerable difficulty in estimating how customers and potential customers will respond to the organization's new e-business functionality. While meeting customer needs is a good business decision, it is difficult to predict and measure the benefit of these improvements. The following are questions to ask when determining the benefits:

- What will be the cost if the organization does not implement the e-business strategy? Will the company fall behind the competition?
- Why is the e-business effort required to support the business strategy?
- What is the estimated impact of improved customer satisfaction?
- How much will sales increase?
- How much will total costs decrease?
- What is the estimated benefit of increased process efficiencies?
- What is the estimated benefit of reduced transaction costs?
- What is the impact of reduced inventory?
- What is the impact of improved market presence, extending market reach?
- What is the impact of improved supplier interface?
- What is the impact on a reduced manufacturing cycle time?
- What is the impact of increased speed of transaction from order to ship?
- What is the impact on decreasing customer support costs?
- What is the impact on overhead costs?
- What are the total estimated benefits?
- What are the unquantifiable or qualitative benefits that will be realized?

The costs and benefits can be identified for groups of related opportunities, as well as for implementing the e-business venture in total. Organizations evaluate the effectiveness of investments in many different ways, including:

- Return on investment analysis
- Pay-back period calculation
- Net present value
- Discounted cash flow
- Strategic business value
- Other methods

Although e-business is definitely a strategic requirement, it must be evaluated in the method that is most familiar to the organization. As part of the overall cost/benefit analysis, it is also important to analyze the risk. Any new product and business venture such as an e-business project will have some associated risks. However, taking risks is essential to moving the business forward and remaining competitive. It is important to identify and recognize the risks in advance. Once the risks are understood, the organization may choose to modify the approach or accept the risks and manage them during the implementation. The risks of the e-business venture should be communicated up the chain of command to management as well as down to the individuals involved in the implementation. Examples of how risks could impact e-business projects include:

- Loss of quality
- Problems of availability and reliability issues
- Increased costs
- Missed deadlines
- Personnel issues including motivation, training, and turnover
- Failure to meet objectives or metrics
- Customer dissatisfaction
- Technology issues
- Impact on the business

Several different categories of risks may be associated with the e-business venture. Ask the following questions:

- Are there risks associated with the development time?
- Are there risks associated with the resources?
- Are there risks associated with the resources required in ongoing support of the organization?
- Are there risks associated with the scope of the project?
- Are there risks associated with tasks that cannot be easily measured?
- What is the greatest risk, delay in implementation or accuracy and completeness of a Web site?

When analyzing the risks associated with time consider:

- Tasks in the development process that take longer than a few weeks or more than 10% of the total development cycle time
- Tasks on the critical path of the development
- Tasks with several predecessors
- Tasks that are overly complex
- Tasks that are extremely variable in time
- Tasks with tight time frames
- Tasks with unrealistic time estimates
- Availability of resources to meet the development and implementation time frames
- New technology requiring time for a proof-of-concept process
- Ability to change business processes in the allocated time

When analyzing risks relative to resources look for:

- Tasks that require substantial resources
- Tasks that require a specific skill set or scarce skill set
- Tasks heavily dependent on one person
- Tasks that rely on external resources or groups
- Limited availability of tools or automation to support the tasks
- Risks associated with the technology
- Acceptance of the new technology and processes
- Availability of resources for the development and implementation
- Availability of resources for the ongoing support and maintenance
- Change management issues

Risks relative to scope include:

- Tasks of the process that interface with the business
- Tasks that are critical to meet performance metrics identified
- Tasks that rely on business input, areas outside of direct control
- Tasks required by external organizations or partners
- Tasks that are too large and take too long to complete
- Tasks that are difficult to measure

Effective management involves proactively managing the risks and implementing strategies to deal with the risks. As shown in Figure 7.13, there are three different strategies:

- **Reduce the risk:** Reduce the probability that the situation will happen or minimize the impact the risk will have

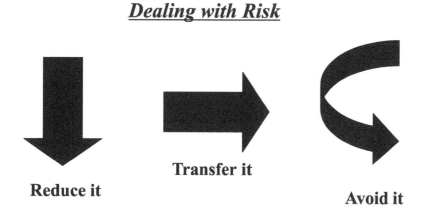

Dealing with Risk

Transfer it

Reduce it

Avoid it

Figure 7.13   Dealing with Risk

- **Transfer the risk:** Move or shift the risk to another area or party; although this does not avoid or reduce the risk, it is one way that individuals choose to deal with risk
- **Avoid the risk:** Take a different action completely, with less risk

With any new direction, there are challenges and risks. Effective risk management can be used to mitigate the impact of the risk. To mitigate the areas of risk:

- Design redundancy into the process
- Add resources
- Cross-train resources
- Schedule high-risk tasks early in the process
- Have proper controls or reviews in place for the high-risk areas
- Eliminate high-risk tasks
- Prototype or test the new process
- Add or remove technology

Steps to manage risk are shown in Figure 7.14. They include:

1. State the risk. What could go wrong? Clearly state the risk so it is understood and can be managed properly. Identify the cause, condition, and consequences of the risk.
2. Identify who is responsible for managing the risk.
3. Identify the probability of the risk happening. This could be a numeric value for high (3), medium (2), or low (1), or it could be a percent likelihood of happening (e.g., 75%, 50%).
4. Identify the impact or severity of the risk. This impact could be identified as high (3), medium (2), or low (1).
5. Identify the overall exposure of the risk. Multiply the probability times the impact to determine the overall exposure. The risks can be prioritized by the overall exposure. You may choose to ignore the risks with low exposure, as they may not be worth the effort to manage.
6. Identify the plans to prevent or minimize the risk.
7. Identify contingency plans if the risk occurs and trigger appropriate action should it occur and who is responsible for implementing the plan should the need arise.

Ensure that the risk management, control, and metrics are integrated into the overall design of the e-business development process. Understand the degree of change that is necessary to implement e-business.

Now draft the costs, benefits, and return on investment sections of your e-business plan document.

Risk	Responsible	Probability	Impact	Exposure	Prevention Plan	Contingency Plan
IS personnel turnover	Sue Adams	3	1	3	Listen, IS satisfaction survey and actions	New employee training plan
Technology difficult to use	Ben Smith	3	2	6	Test and train in new technology	Evaluate technology options
Technology not working	Ben Smith	1	3	3	Test and train in new technology	Evaluate technology options
Technology not perfect fit for process	Ben Smith	2	2	4	Test and train in new technology	Evaluate technology options
Customers don't like process	Andy Johnson	1	3	3	Communication to customers	Modify process
IS process participants not trained	Sue Adams	1	3	3	Training	Training
IS process participants don't like new process	Sue Adams	2	1	2	Training, communication	Listen, modify process
Lack of resources to implement	Andy Johnson	2	2	4	Management commitment	Modify process
Lack of resources for ongoing operation	Andy Johnson	2	3	6	Management commitment	Modify process
Issues with interfaces to other processes	Andy Johnson	2	2	4	Test process	Modify process
Metrics get worse rather than better	Andy Johnson	1	2	2	Pilot	Analyze, modify process
Documentation gets out of date	Sue Adams	3	2	6	Periodic review of documentation	Update documentation
Process doesn't work	Andy Johnson	1	3	3	Test process, pilot	Analyze, modify process

Note for probability, Impact: high = 3, medium = 2, low = 1

Figure 7.14   Risk Management

ROADMAP

A roadmap is a migration path of clear and manageable projects of reasonable size that move the company toward the strategic direction. It takes into consideration not only the goal, but also the organizational constraints and balances cost, benefits, and risk. It is important not to take on too much for the organization, or e-business will fail.

Chapter 6 (Phase 4) identified several different methods for prioritizing opportunities. After identifying the costs and benefits, review the priorities that were identified to see if any changes are necessary based on the cost/benefit and risk analysis that was completed. Take opportunities that are not possible or would provide little value, and move them to a separate list for re-evaluation at a later date. If there are many opportunities, group the opportunities into projects by addressing opportunities that impact the same business process or business application area. The business or customers should identify what to develop by prioritizing the e-business projects, and the Information Systems organization should identify how to implement the opportunities. The following are considerations when determining priorities and e-business projects:

- Identify first efforts and low-hanging fruit to help get the e-business strategy moving and producing results. It helps to communicae to the organization that the business is serious about e-business and is moving toward success.
- It is important to identify opportunities that can be achieved in a 3- to 5-month time frame, or less.
- Identify efforts that can achieve a payback that is greater than the cost of the project within 1 year.
- Minimize risk, cost, and time by selecting proven solutions from proven vendors. Select companies who have successfully implemented the solution elsewhere.
- The industry and customer desires are continually changing, so the roadmap should continually be reviewed for changes in priority.

The following are questions to consider when developing the roadmap:

- How much money can the organization afford to spend per year on e-business?
- How quickly must the organization achieve the strategic vision?
- How well can the organization implement and adapt to change?
- What opportunities will achieve the greatest benefit?
- Are projects scheduled for completion in 3 to 5 months or less?

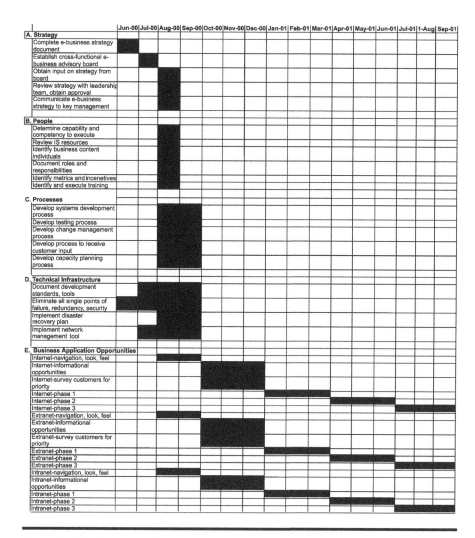

	Jun-00	Jul-00	Aug-00	Sep-00	Oct-00	Nov-00	Dec-00	Jan-01	Feb-01	Mar-01	Apr-01	May-01	Jun-01	Jul-01	1-Aug	Sep-01
A. Strategy																
Complete e-business strategy document	■															
Establish cross-functional e-business advisory board		■														
Obtain input on strategy from board			■													
Review strategy with leadership team, obtain approval			■													
Communicate e-business strategy to key management			■													
B. People																
Determine capability and competency to execute			■													
Review IS resources			■													
Identify business content individuals			■													
Document roles and responsibilities			■													
Identify metrics and incenetives			■													
Identify and execute training			■													
C. Processes																
Develop systems development process			■	■												
Develop testing process			■													
Develop change management process			■													
Develop process to receive customer input			■													
Develop capacity planning process			■													
D. Technical Infrastructure																
Document development standards, tools		■	■	■												
Eliminate all single points of failure, redundancy, security			■	■												
Implement disaster recovery plan		■														
Implement network management tool			■													
E. Business Application Opportunities																
Internet-navigation, look, feel				■												
Internet-informational opportunities						■										
Internet-survey customers for priority					■											
Internet-phase 1								■								
Internet-phase 2											■					
Internet-phase 3														■		
Extranet-navigation, look, feel				■												
Extranet-informational opportunities						■										
Extranet-survey customers for priority					■											
Extranet-phase 1								■								
Extranet-phase 2											■					
Extranet-phase 3														■		
Intranet-navigation, look, feel				■												
Intranet-informational opportunities						■										
Intranet-phase 1								■								
Intranet-phase 2											■					
Intranet-phase 3														■		

Figure 7.15 Roadmap Summary

■ Does each project have a defined deliverable, with a beginning and an end?

■ Will the initial projects provide a positive momentum for the e-business effort?

■ Will the initial projects provide a payback greater than the cost of the project within 1 year?

Figure 7.15 shows an example of a roadmap summary.
Now draft the roadmap section of your e-business plan document.

APPROVAL

Even the best-drafted plans are not effective if not approved by executive management for execution. It is critical that throughout the planning process, executive management is actively involved in the development and formation of the plan. If management is involved throughout the process, the approval step can be very easy and uneventful.

Begin by summarizing the entire plan in the executive summary section of the plan document. Each section of the plan can be summarized in a few sentences. Address the following questions:

- Why is e-business critical for the company?
- What is happening in the industry to warrant concern?
- What is the current status of e-business for the company?
- How does the current state of e-business compare with competition?
- Are there major changes planned to the value chain?
- What are major changes to the business plan?
- Who are the customers?
- What is the value proposition?
- What is a summary of the e-business strategy?
- What is the total number of e-business opportunities that were identified?
- What is the total cost of the e-business projects? What is the cost over the next year? 2 years?
- What is the total benefit of the e-business projects?
- What is the return on investment?
- What can the company expect to accomplish with e-business?

Now draft the executive summary section of your e-business plan document. After completing the executive summary, distribute the e-business plan document to executive management for review. Hold a presentation to summarize, discuss, and gain approval of the plan. You are now done with the e-business planning phases. After obtaining approval, you are ready to begin the first of the implementation stages, the design phase.

KEY POINTS TO REMEMBER

- To e-enable an enterprise, it is important that the business applications are fully integrated in an enterprise framework.
- System reliability, availability, performance, scalability, flexibility, and security are all key considerations when designing the technical architecture.

- Simplify, standardize, integrate, and automate the technical infrastructure.
- Well-defined and seamless business processes are required for an efficient e-enabled organization and value chain.
- Information systems processes should be reviewed and re-engineered to meet the e-business requirements.
- E-business also impacts the organization structures, culture, job responsibilities, and titles of individuals. Remember to recognize and manage the human components to the changes required for e-business.
- If a service provider is necessary, selection and careful review are critical to the organization's e-business success.
- Although e-business is a strategic requirement, a thorough review of the costs, benefits, and return on investment is important for prudent management.
- Identify and manage risks associated with e-business.
- The roadmap should be a list of clear and manageable projects of reasonable size that balance cost, benefits, and risk for the organization.
- Involve executive management actively throughout the formation of the e-business plan as it will help significantly in the approval stages.

NOTES FOR MY E-BUSINESS EFFORT

8

PHASE 6—DESIGN

"Knowledge resides in the user and not in the collection. It's how the user reacts to the collection that really matters."

C. West Churchman

The sixth phase of e-business is to **Design**, the beginning of the implementation of the e-business plan and strategy that has been developed in Phases 1 through 5. As shown in Figure 8.1, in this phase, you will design the overall look and feel of the Web site, navigation, screens, applications, and security.

LOOK AND FEEL

Designing the overall look and feel that the organization wants to portray with its e-business presence is critical. Many organizations spend millions of dollars selecting a company logo, company colors, business cards, and marketing brochures, and pay little attention to the messages their Web sites convey. An organization's Web presence and design are as important, or more important, than many other methods to communicate a company image and message.

The first visible component of a site's look and feel is the actual domain name itself. Keep the domain name short, intuitive, easy to spell, memorable, and related to the business or company name. Although the domain name can be up to 67 characters long, shorter is usually better. Begin with the organization's name, motto, or field of business. Look at ways the organization's name can be shortened to a few key words or acronyms. Also be sure to buy alternative domain names that the customer is likely to think of when trying to get to the organization's site. Reserve additional

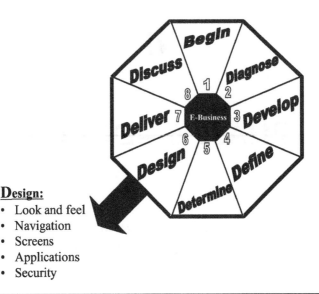

Design:
- Look and feel
- Navigation
- Screens
- Applications
- Security

Figure 8.1   Phase 6, Design

extensions or misspellings that might also be used. On November 16, 2000, the Internet Corporation for Assigned Names and Numbers (ICANN, www.icann.org), the authority that governs global Internet domain names, approved seven new domain extensions in addition to .com, .net, and .org. These are the first new global Internet domains approved by ICANN in over a decade. They are:

- .biz: businesses
- .info: unrestricted use
- .name: registration by individuals
- .pro: accountants, lawyers, and physicians
- .aero: air-transport industry
- .coop: cooperatives
- .museum: museums

As new extensions will be added, be sure someone in the organization has the responsibility to reserve additional related domains and renew domains as necessary. There are many sites to help develop domain names (such as www.nameboy.com, www.networksolutions.com NameFetcher, www.e-gineer.com Domainator) and register the domain. www.internic.net has a listing of all the accredited registrars of domains.

Good design and good looks matter. A good design can make a Web site stand out among its competitors. It can boost traffic and sales, and keep customers coming back. Every impression or visitor is a sales opportunity or loss. In e-business, it is critical to attract customers, keep them, and keep them coming back. If customers go to the Web site and things are not easy to find, they can get frustrated. Remember they are just one click away from a competitor.

When designing the overall look and feel of the Web site, first consider the customer, or the audience the organization is trying to attract to the Web site. Review the results of Phase 2 (Chapter 4) when stakeholders were identified. Who is the customer? Select a design that the customer would find attractive. Is the customer:

- High-tech
- Low-tech
- Professional, white-collar worker
- Craftsman, blue-collar worker
- Conservative, cost conscious, frugal
- Security conscious
- Trendy
- Traditional
- Flamboyant, high profile, desiring attention
- Quiet, low profile, desiring anonymity

Understand the needs of the audience. Define the value the organization's site is going to provide the user. Review the value proposition that was developed in Phase 3 (Chapter 5). Is the customer looking for information, convenience, learning, or communication? Provide the right content for the right audience. For example:

- Business users have a very focused information need.
- Convenience shoppers want to make a transaction quickly.
- Surfers are looking for recreation and information.
- Learners are looking for in-depth information and training courses.
- Wireless users are looking for efficiency in downloading.

General guidelines when designing the Web site include:

- Have the company logo clearly visible on each page.
- Keep content current.
- Have an archive of previously published content.
- Minimize the need to scroll.
- Structure content into hierarchies, but don't make it too complex.
- Use the technology to listen. Build the site so it has the capability for continuous user feedback.

■ Use up-selling, cross-selling, and re-selling opportunities whenever possible.

■ Use tools to support the design whenever possible. Tools such as Flash from Macromedia Inc. allow animation to be added to a site. However, be aware that required software downloads to enable your Web site may turn people away. Other products help with search functions, such as Excite Inc's search engine and advanced search tools from companies such as Ask Jeeves Inc. and Google Inc. Personalization systems from Blue Martini Software Inc. and BroadVision Inc. assist with individualization. Links can also be built to customer service representatives for live conversations with customer service agents using software such as LivePerson.com Inc.

Consider the following questions about the design:

■ Is there something on the main page to get the customer's attention and engage interest? How can the organization capture and seduce the intended audience?

■ How can the organization establish a positive relationship? How can it be a comfortable experience for the customer?

■ How can the organization get customers to come back? How can it be memorable?

■ How can the organization create a meaningful personal relationship?

■ Does the site invite the customers, welcome them, and help them to be effective?

■ Does the design enhance and communicate the corporate image and establish the organization's brand?

NAVIGATION

The navigation is the road map of the site. If visitors find the site's navigation confusing, they will give up and go somewhere else. Good navigation is an essential ingredient for any Web site. Go back to the customer and stakeholders' processes that were outlined in Phase 2 (Chapter 4). Consider organizing the navigation and content in the process in which the customer will use the information.

The following are guidelines for navigation:

■ Put the search and contact us functions in an easy-to-find spot on every screen.

■ Avoid navigation that takes the customer away from the site.

■ Establish a home page and always provide a clear path back home.

■ Label buttons clearly and concisely.

- Be consistent.
- Always give visitors a sense of where they are within the navigation.
- Don't take up too much room with navigation; save room for valuable content.
- Keep it simple.

SCREENS

An effective Web site has to be more than just flashy looking. It must be inviting and communicate the information that the visitor is looking to find. The content must be fresh and current. There are two aspects to screen content: what is said and how it is said. Screen design is very subjective. What looks good to one person might not to another person. Again, consider the customer the organization is trying to attract to the site. For example, when contemplating a screen design change, Amazon.com even asked its customers to vote on which design they liked best.

Features to consider in the screen and content design include:

- Colors (background, titles, headlines)
- Typeface
- Layout
- Movement, animation
- Sound
- Graphic accents
- Navigation links
- Performance

Keep graphics and text files small. If the page does not load quickly, the visitor may go somewhere else. Use graphics and other band-width-intensive elements wisely.

Consider the following questions:

- How will the organization reinforce its image?
- How can emphasis be added?
- Is the message as easy to read as possible (i.e., effective use of columns, typeface, type size, alignment, line spacing, white space, punctuation, capitalization, text wraps, word spacing, color)?
- Does the content have the information in which customers would be interested?
- Is the mix of text and graphics or visuals pleasing?
- Does the screen catch the customer's attention or get involvement?
- Does the screen provide the image that the organization wishes to communicate (e.g., conservative, contemporary, cheap, expensive, quiet, dignified, flamboyant, formal, informal)?

- Is the site fresh with some time-sensitive information? Does the site give the users something to come back for?

APPLICATIONS

Designing the business applications behind the flashy Web site is important to keeping a satisfied customer. In Phase 5 (Chapter 7), the business application architecture was determined at a high level. It is now time to design the individual application functions and interfaces. To be e-enabled, the business applications from the front-end to the back-end must be fully integrated.

Questions to consider include:

- Can accurate information be provided to the customer online and quickly?
- How can marketing efforts be automated to improve efficiency?
- How can the sales force processes be automated to improve efficiency?
- How can call centers and customer databases be integrated?
- How can customer responses and profiles be automated, and quotes and proposals be managed throughout the process?
- How can the order management process be automated so the organization is easy to do business with?
- How can a transparent interface be provided to the customer throughout the process from product design to product delivery?
- How can the information flow be improved and overall product costs be reduced by improving the flow of goods through production?
- How can lead times be reduced, quality increased, and customization enabled at a lower cost?
- How can inventory be replaced with improved information?

SECURITY

Security must be designed not only as part of the technical architecture, but also in the business applications. Most infrastructure components fail to provide protection for applications with poorly designed or implemented security. The organization's security program should have several different layers of protection between a potential attacker and critical data and systems. Securing information means preventing corruption and selectively allowing only authorized people to see it. Security is a matter of degree.

Questions to ask regarding security include:

- How likely is a security breach?
- What are the consequences of a security issue or breach?
- How much processing and cost are justified to counter security threats?
- What groups of individuals cannot see other groups of individuals' information? This includes other geographies, other stakeholders, and other partners.
- What information should be secured?
- Are the programmers following secure programming practices?
- Are security policies enforced at the application level before input gets to the e-business software?

Now that the e-business functionality is designed, you are ready to move into the deliver phase.

KEY POINTS TO REMEMBER

- Design the overall look and feel that the organization wants to portray with its e-business presence. Good design and good looks matter.
- Design from the customer vantage point.
- Assign responsibility to reserve additional domain names and renew domains as necessary.
- Consider organizing the navigation by the stakeholders and the stakeholders' process that was identified.
- Design integrated applications behind the e-business screens.
- Design multiple layers of security protection.

NOTES FOR MY E-BUSINESS EFFORT

9

PHASE 7—DELIVER

"The secret of success is constancy to purpose."

Benjamin Disraeli

The seventh phase of the e-business planning process is to **Deliver**. As shown in Figure 9.1, in this phase, you will develop the e-business functionality and environment, test, train, and finally implement. You will then promote the new e-business functionality.

DEVELOP

Although the Internet changes everything, it is still important to follow solid development practices. Good project management is a prerequisite for success. The e-business project is no different from other projects for the organization. The CHAOS study by the Standish Group, which is often cited, found that only 26% of projects were successful.* We need to focus on finding ways to consistently enable good people to deliver quality solutions on time and within budget.

As with any project, it is the job of the project manager to understand the true status of a project, identify and solve any problems as early as possible. Many times, information systems people are optimists, planning that no issues will arise, or because it is technically possible it will be implemented quickly. Good project management techniques and principles are required for e-business projects even more so than traditional information systems projects because time is of the essence. Projects cannot afford to wallow around in a 90% completed status for months

---

* "Will Your Project Survive?" *CIO Magazine*, Section 1, February 15, 1999, p. 42.

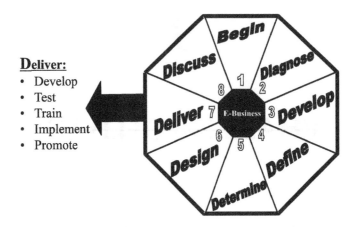

Deliver:
• Develop
• Test
• Train
• Implement
• Promote

Figure 9.1 Phase 7, Deliver

on end. The following are project management and development tips and techniques:

- Ensure the project team is a solid high-performing and well-functioning team. If not, obtain assistance for training or to add resources to the team.
- Clearly identify roles and responsibilities of the project and assign to team members.
- Ensure resources stay committed to the project at the level anticipated throughout the life of the project.
- Make sure the business requirements and customer needs are understood by everyone. Technology is not an end; it is a means to an end.
- Don't sacrifice quality; sacrifice scope. E-business projects must get to market quickly. Learn and adjust. Maintaining quality is crucial, even more so than internal software as it will impact the customer directly. If necessary, break the project into phases to keep the scope manageable.
- Keep the scope realistic and managed. Changes must be controlled.
- As with any project, e-business projects are constrained and have trade-offs of time, cost, and quality. You can only fix or constrain two of the three. If you drive the team to a rigid cost and time, quality will suffer. If you have a set quality and cost, time will suffer. If you have a set time and quality, cost will suffer. Manage and communicate the risks.
- Use a project methodology to ensure the project stays on track and within budget. It doesn't matter particularly which methodology is used; just use one methodology consistently.

- Each project should have a documented project plan with a schedule, identified team, and documented responsibilities. Each e-business project should be planned with small deliverable tasks. Each task should have one person responsible with a planned deliver date. Make deadlines aggressive, but not unrealistic.
- The project plan must consider training and process changes that will be necessary. Consider integration issues to back office and front office systems.
- Ensure that communication is frequent, open, and honest throughout the project team, business, and management.
- Frequently review the status of each task. Ask direct questions and don't allow vague answers. Weekly project management meetings are recommended to review the previous week's deliverables and discuss the deliverables for the next week. Team meetings should be documented. Any issues should be documented and acted upon.
- Use technology that is proven. If it is new, do a proof of concept before beginning a project.
- Whenever possible, utilize vendor-supplied packages rather than writing custom software.
- Model or prototype software whenever possible. This will ensure the development is on track.
- Use an iterative, incremental approach to application development. Have frequent release cycles.
- Whenever possible, use objects or re-useable code that has been tested.
- Use a source code peer-review process.
- Complete post-project reviews to analyze if the business benefits were achieved.

Risk management must be part of the entire design and development process. Trade-offs will continually be made between security, ease-of use, availability, speed to market, quality, performance, and openness. Strike a balance between risk and value. Risk assessment methodologies provide some guidance to making sound e-business trade-off decisions. Consider building multiple Web sites, possibly for different lines of business or different groups of customers to limit the impact of issues. Partition functionality for scalability.

TEST

Testing is critical, particularly as systems are now directly in front of customers. Murphy's Law applies to e-business ventures just like other information systems projects. A poorly tested system can result in bad publicity and unhappy customers, and can even impact the stock. Don't short-cut the testing process to get the system to market. Test, test, and test some more.

Be sure to do a pilot test as well as a stress test. Before doing the pilot or stress test, define acceptable metrics so it is known how success and failure will be measured and judged. The following questions will help check your testing:

- Were all the business processes tested?
- Were connectivity issues tested?
- Were all the locations tested?
- Were any fixes tested?
- Was testing performed on different clients and different hardware?
- Were different browsers and browser releases (Internet Explorer, Netscape Navigator, etc.) tested?
- Were different resolutions (640 × 480, 800 × 600, and 1024 × 768) tested?
- Were different color depths (256, 16-bit, 24-bit) tested?
- Were different operating systems (Windows releases, Mac releases) tested?
- Were different connection speeds (14.4 KB, 56 KB) tested?
- Was security tested?
- Was a stress test completed?
- Was the contingency plan tested?

TRAIN

Do not underestimate the training necessary for your e-business efforts to be a success. E-business projects often involve significant changes for the organization, including process changes, changes in responsibilities, and changes in technology. If the human aspects of any change are overlooked, the most technically proficient solution can be a failure. Consider the following questions:

- Have all the individuals involved in the new business processes been identified?
- Do all the individuals understand their new roles, expectations, and the metrics upon which they will be measured?
- Do all the individuals understand the business direction and priorities and what they mean to them and their jobs?
- Have all the individuals been trained in the new business process?
- Have all the individuals been trained in the new technology?
- Have the Information Systems individuals been trained properly in the new technology?

- Have the Information Systems individuals been trained properly in the new processes?
- Have any organization changes been communicated to the individuals impacted as well as the organization?
- Have procedures and documentation been updated for employees to reference?
- Do you have the acceptance, involvement, and commitment of the organization to make e-business successful?

IMPLEMENT

How exciting that the e-business functionality is ready for implementation! However, this stage must also be accomplished with care. Typically a phased implementation is a good idea so that pieces can be tested in production. If possible, implement well before a major promotion so the site can be tested with normal loads before experiencing heavy spikes. Don't underestimate the training necessary and the impact of the business process changes. Consider the following questions:

- Who will respond to questions that are submitted? What is the process? How quickly will questions be responded to?
- Who will respond to requests for literature and additional information? What is the process? How quickly will requests be responded to? Who will follow up leads for potential sales?
- Who will compile the information received on registration forms and update customer files? What will the information be used for? Is all the information present that is required?
- What are the disaster recovery plan and business continuity plan? Have they been tested?
- Does the culture support the business objectives of customer satisfaction?
- Has the organization invested in proactive capacity planning and change simulation tools?
- Has the organization invested in real-time availability and performance management tools?
- As volume cannot be predicted, is excess capacity maintained? Is load balancing in place with the ability to add more capacity as needed?
- Has the architecture been planned to enable scheduled downtime for portions of the system while minimizing overall impact?
- Is there no single point of failure, including the technical architecture, applications, people, or processes? Has redundancy been designed?

PROMOTE

Do not expect customers just to find the site; it must be promoted. With 235,000 sites added each month, the organization must ensure its Internet presence receives the exposure necessary for a successful launch. The company must develop a marketing strategy that is consistent with the brand and image. IMT Strategies identified how people get to sites:

- Search engines 43.5%
- Word of mouth 20.2%
- Random surfing 19.9%
- E-mail messages 8.6%
- By accident 2.1%
- Publications 1.4%
- Web browser 1.0%
- Don't know 0.7%
- Radio 0.4%
- Other 0.8%

If the organization wants people to find its site, it must show up near the top of the major search engines. Position the site favorably on search engines (www.webposition.com, www.goto.com). A good resource for search engines is www.searchenginewatch.com. Each search engine has different characteristics and different requirements. Learn and adhere to the criteria for the major search engines. Increasing the relevancy of the site in search engines can be done by:

- Using a descriptive and enticing title for each page with key phrases of 5 to 8 words that will show up in search engine results.
- Incorporating key phrases into the description, as well as any other important words.
- Placing the description on top of the Web page between header tags.
- Titling each page appropriately and descriptively rather than putting the same title on all pages. Titles should be high on the page. Tables, columns, and JavaScript push text further down the page, making keywords less relevant.
- Using meta tags that are special text in the <HEAD> section of a Web page. They are read by search engines and are used to figure out what is most important. Usually only the first 75 to 150 characters will be displayed.
- Ensuring the meta tags are relevant to the content. Consider common misspellings.
- Avoiding excessive repeating of any particular word in the meta keywords tag as that could actually downgrade the page.

- Having good content.
- Having visible HTML text on the page, not just graphics, because search engines cannot read graphics.
- Having other sites linking to the site.
- Having HTML hyperlinks to the home page that lead to major sections of the Web site. A search engine may not be able to follow image map links and may miss some valuable descriptions. Having good links internally between pages will help.
- Suggesting the proper category and subcategory when submitting the Web site.
- Having a site map page with text links to everything in the Web site. This can be submitted to help search engines locate pages.
- Following specific submission rules for each site.
- Avoiding symbols in the URLs as some search engines have difficulty with symbols such as the "?".
- Regularly reviewing search engine placement and those of competitors.
- Avoiding spamming search engines as they can be detected and penalized.

Submit to many different search engines. As there are over 1,000 search engines, and the number continues to grow, focus on those most popular. Some of the search engines are:

- AltaVista (www.altavista.com)
- AOL Search (www.search.aol.com)
- AskJeeves (www.askjeeves.com)
- Directhit (www.directhit.com)
- Dogpile (www.dogpile.com)
- Excite (www.excite.com)
- Fastsearch (www.alltheweb.com)
- Google (www.google.com)
- GoTo (www.goto.com)
- HotBot (www.hotbot.com)
- Infoseek (www.infoseek.com)
- Iwon (www.iwon.com)
- LookSmart (www.looksmart.com)
- Lycos (www.lycos.com)
- MSN Search (www.search.msn.com)
- NBCi (www.nbci.com)
- Netscape (www.netscape.com)
- Northern Light (www.northernlight.com)
- WebCrawler (www.webcrawler.com)
- Yahoo (www.yahoo.com)

Consider using submission services such as www.submitit.linkexchange.com, www.netcreations.com/postmaster, or www.all4one.com/all4submit. These services will automatically submit your site to many of the search engines.

Additional promotion possibilities include:

- Put the URL everywhere: on all marketing literature, presentations, business cards, brochures, e-mail signatures, invoices, communications, annual report, letters, news releases, radio ads, television ads, directories, voice mail, side of van, side of building.
- Add the URL to the voice mail system as an option for customers.
- Leverage alliances by cross promotions and links.
- Try to get or purchase links from industry sites.
- Find complementary Web sites and try to establish reciprocal links.
- Begin an affiliate program that has a financial stake in promoting your site (www.cj.com, www.affiliatezone.com).
- Try joining an e-mall service (such as Yahoo).
- Promote the site in mailing lists and news groups (use www.deja-news.com to find sources).
- Join a banner exchange program (such as http://www.linkexchange.com, http://bannertips.com/exchangenetworks.shtml) or purchase banner advertising.
- Purchase advertising in e-mail newsletters.
- Rent targeted e-mail lists, but avoid sending bulk untargeted and unsolicited e-mail.
- Prepare a handout, mailing insert, and e-mail announcement to promote the Web site.
- Make media announcements.

Also consider promotion when designing the site. Give visitors a reason to come back to the site. The following are some design possibilities:

- Try to capture visitor e-mail address and request permission to send updates or newsletters. Ask only for information that is really needed or those contacted will not provide any information.
- Offer special promotions, coupons, and discounts through proactive e-mail messages. Various software packages will take customer information from a database and merge it into e-mails include:
  — Microsoft Office 2000 (www.microsoft.com)
  — MessageMedia MailKing (www.mailking.com)
  — MailWorkz Bro@dcast (www.mailworkz.com)
  — ArialSoft Campaign 2000 (www.arialsoftware.com)
  — Cory Rudl's Mailloop (www.marketingtips.com)
  — Gammadyne Mailer (www.gammadyne.com)

- Think about offering something free or having a contest on the site to entice visitors.
- Ask visitors to bookmark the site, which makes it easy to return.
- Use marketing promotion techniques to help visitors spread the word about the site. For example, offer free e-mail service or a discount if they e-mail the site to a friend.

Make sure that someone within the organization has the responsibility for promotion and marketing, as it must be an ongoing task.

KEY POINTS TO REMEMBER

- Solid development practices and good project management are prerequisites for e-business success.
- Don't sacrifice quality; sacrifice scope. Get to market fast; learn and adjust.
- Understand trade-offs of time, cost, and quality. Risk management should be part of the development process.
- Use a project methodology with project plans, small deliverable efforts, assigned responsibilities, and delivery dates.
- Don't short-cut the testing process to get to market quicker. Test, test, and test some more.
- Don't underestimate the training necessary and the impact of the business process changes during implementation.
- The e-business site and functionality must be proactively promoted.

NOTES FOR MY E-BUSINESS EFFORT

10

PHASE 8—DISCUSS

"Far better it is to dare mighty things, to win glorious triumphs, even though checkered by failure ... than to rank with those poor spirits who neither enjoy much nor suffer much, because they live in a gray twilight that knows not victory nor defeat."

Theodore Roosevelt

The eighth and final phase is to **Discuss**. As shown in Figure 10.1, in this phase you will obtain feedback, analyze, and determine the appropriate action. Because e-business is an ongoing effort, with rapid changes in the industry, it is probably appropriate to begin the planning process anew after completion of this phase.

OBTAIN FEEDBACK

Build into the culture the ability to accept failure as a part of growth. Not everything that is implemented will work. Just like downhill skiing, in order to improve you need to take a few falls. If you aren't falling, you aren't pushing yourself to improve. If something isn't working, acknowledge it and change—quickly.

Although the final judge as to the success or failure of your e-business venture is business profitability, a key ingredient to profitability is if the customer likes and wants to use the e-business functionality. Get input and feedback from customers. However, be ready to take action on customer feedback. The following are some ways to obtain customer feedback:

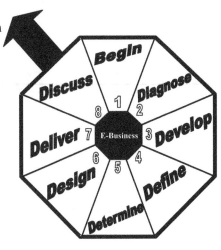

Discuss:
- Obtain feedback
- Analyze
- Determine action

Figure 10.1 Phase 8—Discuss

- Ask them
- Have them respond to an online survey and provide incentive or rewards
- Form a customer user group or forum

In addition to obtaining customer input, review your own site. Consider it from the vantage point of the customer. The following are questions to consider:

- Does the initial screen catch the customer's interest?
- What do customers think of the Internet screens and functionality?
- Do the Internet pages download quickly?
- Are there reasons for visitors to register at the site?
- Is quality of content good?
- Is content up to date and fresh?
- Can visitors find the information they need?
- Is the site organized so the customer can use it easily?
- Can visitors search for information?
- Is it easy for visitors to contact the company?
- Which pages are used the most and least? Is this what was expected?

ANALYZE

There are many tools available on the Internet to analyze Web sites and provide information. For example, software from WebTrends Corp. (www.webtrends.com) can help understand the behavior of potential customers, track what is happening on the site, and detect where customers are dropping off. You may find that customers are leaving the site with items in a shopping cart and not proceeding to check out. Analyze why this might be happening. WebCriteria (www.webcriteria) provides a Web site analysis service. A product called Gif Wizard (www.gifwizard.com) can provide an efficiency analysis. Another example is Alexa (www.alexa.com), which provides free software that can be downloaded to help analyze your Web site as well as the competitor's. Alexa will:

- Identify which Web sites and businesses are worth advertising or partnering with
- Identify competitors and potential partners
- Identify how much traffic the Web site gets and how much competitors' Web sites get
- Helps see which pages on competitor Web sites are most visited so you can ensure you have similar functionality
- Identify other sites that have links to your site
- Find out what customers are saying about your Web site as well as the competitors' sites
- Identify the contact information for sites
- Identify the speed ratings of the site

Go back to the original e-business plan that was created in Phases 1 through 5 and analyze how well the objectives were met. Ask the following questions:

- Did the organization achieve the objectives that were stated in the Executive Summary, Introduction, Strategy, and Benefits sections?
- How does the organization rate now on the e-business scorecard originally developed in the Situation Analysis section?
- Is the organization achieving the metrics and targets that were identified in the Strategy section?
- What benefits were realized that were not identified in the plan?
- What expected benefits were not realized? Why not?
- Were the projects completed on time, within budget, and delivering the planned functionality?
- What problems were encountered?
- What should be changed next time?

Additional questions include:

- What do customers request that is not currently provided?
- What, if anything, has changed in the market?
- How have competitors reacted?
- Does the e-business strategy require changes?
- What new functionality do competitors offer?
- Are performance, availability, and security sufficient?
- Are business processes functioning properly?
- Is site content being updated?
- What new technology developments could be useful?
- Now that the organization has a better understanding of e-business, are there additional revenue opportunities or cost savings that were not originally identified?

It may also be helpful to regularly analyze the results of e-business by completing a scorecard as shown in Exhibit 10.1.

DETERMINE ACTION

The newly designed technical architecture will rapidly fall into disrepair without proper maintenance and administration. The infrastructure will need to be updated for new releases of hardware and software. It should be a priority to stay on top of bug lists and apply patches and new releases by vendors. Improvements and changes will continuously need to be made to your e-business environment. Creating an e-enterprise must be an iterative, rapid fire, but planned process. Consider changes in customer requirements and desires as well as technology changes. On a regular basis, go back through the e-business planning processing to evaluate changes or develop an updated e-business strategy.

KEY POINTS TO REMEMBER

- Build into the culture the ability to accept failure as a part of growth.
- If something isn't working, acknowledge it and change—quickly.
- The customer is the best judge of the success or failure of e-business ventures. Obtain feedback.
- Analyze the functioning of the site. Analyze how well the original objectives were met.
- Allocate sufficient resources to continually maintain and update the e-business environment. Consider changes in customer requirements and technology.

Exihibit 10.1   E-Business Results Scorecard

		Rating
1.	A majority of customers can be reached or influenced in less than 1 hour	1 2 3 4 5
2.	We proactively maintain electronic communications with the majority of our customers	1 2 3 4 5
3.	A majority of customers utilize our Internet functions on a regular basis	1 2 3 4 5
4.	The following functions are provided to customers via the Internet:	
	■ Advertising, promotion	1 2 3 4 5
	■ Product search and information	1 2 3 4 5
	■ Custom configuration	1 2 3 4 5
	■ Order acceptance and acknowledgment	1 2 3 4 5
	■ Credit checking	1 2 3 4 5
	■ Order scheduling	1 2 3 4 5
	■ Availability checking	1 2 3 4 5
	■ Product shipping	1 2 3 4 5
	■ Payment and funds transfer	1 2 3 4 5
	■ Customer support	1 2 3 4 5
	■ Feedback	1 2 3 4 5
5.	Customer satisfaction of Internet services is high	1 2 3 4 5
6.	The Internet has had a direct impact on sales	1 2 3 4 5
7.	The Internet has had an indirect impact on sales	1 2 3 4 5
8.	The Internet has had an overall positive impact on customer satisfaction	1 2 3 4 5
9.	The Internet has increased customer retention	1 2 3 4 5
10.	The Internet has enabled revenue in new markets	1 2 3 4 5
11.	The Internet has increased market share	1 2 3 4 5
12.	The Internet has provided a competitive advantage in the market	1 2 3 4 5
13.	An Extranet is available to partners to facilitate business-to-business transactions	1 2 3 4 5
14.	The following functions are provided to suppliers and partners via the Extranet:	
	■ Order or demand visibility	1 2 3 4 5
	■ Purchase requisition and order	1 2 3 4 5
	■ Payment and funds transfer	1 2 3 4 5
	■ Supplier delivery and performance information	1 2 3 4 5
15.	A large percent of employees are involved in some way with the Internet, Intranet, or Extranet	1 2 3 4 5

Exihibit 10.1   E-Business Results Scorecard (continued)

16. The following areas have processes enabled by Intranet-
     based applications:
     ■ Marketing   1 2 3 4 5
     ■ Sales   1 2 3 4 5
     ■ Research and Development   1 2 3 4 5
     ■ Manufacturing   1 2 3 4 5
     ■ Procurement   1 2 3 4 5
     ■ Support and Services   1 2 3 4 5
     ■ Human Resources   1 2 3 4 5
     ■ Finance   1 2 3 4 5
     ■ Information Systems   1 2 3 4 5
     ■ General Administration   1 2 3 4 5
17. The Intranet is utilized regularly by the majority of   1 2 3 4 5
     employees
18. The Intranet has enabled faster and more accurate   1 2 3 4 5
     decisions
19. The Intranet has decreased time to market   1 2 3 4 5
20. The Extranet and Intranet have directly reduced costs   1 2 3 4 5
21. The Extranet and Intranet have indirectly reduced costs   1 2 3 4 5
22. We have measured positive return on investment from the   1 2 3 4 5
     majority of e-business projects
23. The majority of e-business projects have been completed   1 2 3 4 5
     on time, within budget, delivering the necessary
     functionality
24. We have experienced minimal security intrusions   1 2 3 4 5
25. We have experienced no down-time or service impact   1 2 3 4 5

NOTES FOR MY E-BUSINESS EFFORT

11

SUMMARY

"You must have long-range goals to keep you from being frustrated by short-range failures."

Charles C. Noble

METHODOLOGY OVERVIEW

Congratulations! You have now made it through the complete e-business methodology as outlined in Figure 11.1. Looking back at your journey, you **began** in Phase 1 by obtaining executive support, identifying the purpose of the e-business initiative, and identifying the team and the planning process. A communication plan was identified to keep the organization up to date, and the e-business effort was announced to the organization. In Phase 2, you **diagnosed** industry trends and the current situation. Stakeholders and their process were identified. You reviewed the value chain and the business situation. In Phase 3, you **developed** the value proposition, value delivery, e-business strategy, and metrics to measure success. In Phase 4, you **defined** specific e-business opportunities, reviewed the competitive situation in detail, and identified initial priorities. In Phase 5, you **determined** the impact to the application architecture, technical architecture, business processes, information systems processes, and people. You outlined the cost/benefit analysis and the roadmap, and obtained approval of the e-business plan. You now had a complete e-business plan as shown by the table of contents sample in Appendix B. In Phase 6, you **designed** the look and feel, navigation, screens, applications, and security. In Phase 7, you **delivered** the e-business functionality by developing the systems, testing, implementing, and promoting the new e-business functionality. In Phase 8, you **discussed** the results of the e-business effort by obtaining and analyzing feedback, and determining the appropriate action.

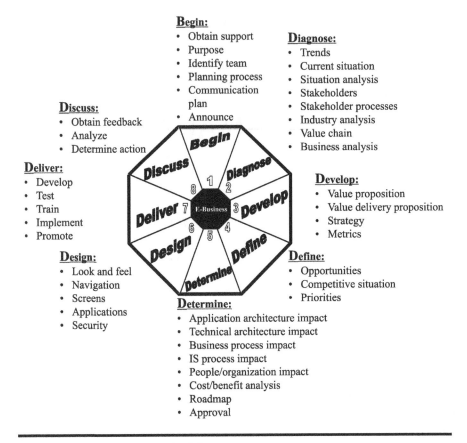

Begin:
- Obtain support
- Purpose
- Identify team
- Planning process
- Communication plan
- Announce

Diagnose:
- Trends
- Current situation
- Situation analysis
- Stakeholders
- Stakeholder processes
- Industry analysis
- Value chain
- Business analysis

Discuss:
- Obtain feedback
- Analyze
- Determine action

Deliver:
- Develop
- Test
- Train
- Implement
- Promote

Develop:
- Value proposition
- Value delivery proposition
- Strategy
- Metrics

Design:
- Look and feel
- Navigation
- Screens
- Applications
- Security

Define:
- Opportunities
- Competitive situation
- Priorities

Determine:
- Application architecture impact
- Technical architecture impact
- Business process impact
- IS process impact
- People/organization impact
- Cost/benefit analysis
- Roadmap
- Approval

Figure 11.1   E-Business Methodology

Following this process provides an organization with many of the components necessary for success. It helps you design an e-business strategy from the outside in, from the customer vantage point.

SUCCESS CRITERIA

E-business has made the transition from a competitive advantage to a requirement. E-business is no longer a question of **whether**, but **how** and is rapidly becoming woven into the fabric of all business enterprises. Truly e-enabling an enterprise is much more than having an Internet site, it is integrating people, processes, and technology to transform the entire business model. As shown in Figure 11.2, the following are keys to successfully e-enabling an enterprise:

■ **Identify a clear e-business leader:** E-business must be owned by the business. It is a business project, not a technology project. Executive leadership and vision are critical to e-business success.

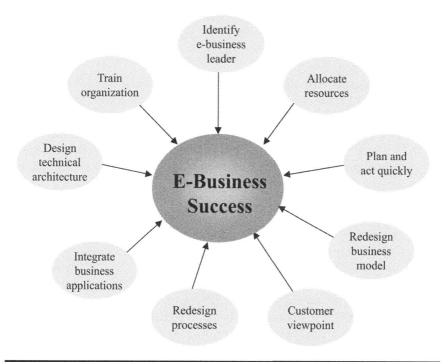

Figure 11.2   E-Business Success

- **Allocate the resources:** E-enabling an enterprise is a large effort that will take financial and human investment throughout the entire process. The effort must be recognized as a major business initiative with the proper resources allocated to be successful.
- **Plan and act quickly:** The world is moving fast. Business agility is key to success. Organizations must learn to react quickly and take advantage of opportunities before the environment changes. A clearly stated and readily understood strategy can help the company react quickly and decisively when the unexpected strikes and changes occur. And changes will occur! Competition and opportunities will come from places not even dreamed of today. Companies must transform to lean and agile companies that anticipate and quickly react to change. Companies that are best positioned to adapt to the fast-moving changes are those that know their customers, know their business, plan accordingly, act quickly, and change as necessary. If a factor in the industry is highly dynamic, and the organization is not flexible in that aspect, it is a threat to the organization's survival. If, on the other hand, the organization is very flexible in a particular area that is slow to change in the industry, it may represent a significant opportunity

and competitive advantage where the organization can change the rules of the game. Let goals drive metrics, and measure progress. Plan flexible infrastructures. Focus and prioritize efforts. Start small, plan big, and go fast!

■ **Redesign the business model:** The rules are changing in the new economy. The companies that will survive are those that go back to the business fundamentals to clearly identify core competencies and value propositions. E-business is about business. The business must be transformed to create new forms of value. Becoming an e-enabled enterprise requires organizations to think and act differently than they have in the past. Successful companies will proactively take advantage of new business opportunities rather than responding reactively to competitive threats. This requires rigorous business planning to identify and create new opportunities to exploit. Technology is a means to a clearly defined business strategy, not an end in itself. Without a clear business strategy, technology will drive the business rather than the business driving technology. Take advantage of the strengths of the business and mold the business into what customers want. Consider the impact of the new networked web of value and extended enterprises enabled by the Internet rather than old sequential value chains. By integrating the entire value chain, the power of the value chain is greater than the sum of the individual organizations. In the new world of interconnected value chains, operate multiple companies as though they were one, realign systems and culture to support cooperation, and create business strategies that exploit the power of the entire value chain. Although the Internet is a great tool to connect companies, the rules of business must be redesigned. There are often boundaries between departments, geographies and divisions, in addition to separate companies and competitors. These changes require a different technical architecture, culture, business processes, and business strategy. Conventional assumptions are no longer valid. Identify what the company does best, port it to the Internet, and obtain the rest from a networked web of partners. The e-business strategy must be identified so different business channels complement each other rather than conflict with each other.

■ **Design from the customer viewpoint:** The customer should be at the top of every organization chart. The customer has the power in the new economy and drives the organization. Just as relationships are built through listening and responding, so are e-business strategies developed by listening to the needs of stakeholders and implementing accordingly. Use the technology to listen to customers. Progressive companies find innovative ways to reach out to their customers.

Learn from these companies, even if they are in different industries. Find out who your customers are and what they want, and forge strong relationships with them. Customer satisfaction is the main metric in the new economy. Manage the organization and design the e-business strategy from the customer vantage point. Be a customer-led organization.

■ **Redesign the processes:** The single largest challenge to e-enabling an enterprise is redesigning business processes. New processes must be designed for efficiency, reliability, and flexibility to be true e-processes. Existing processes in many companies require trained employees. Often, applications and business process are designed for those trained employees rather than an end customer. Adding a Web site on top of bad processes merely advertises how bad they are. Both business and information systems processes must be redesigned for the new environment. The entire information flow within a value chain should be redesigned. Cross-functional teams should be in place to continuously improve processes. E-business and the Internet are an enabling technology, but the true value cannot be realized until business processes are redesigned and new ways of working are adopted.

■ **Integrate the business applications:** Flexibility, integration, and responsiveness are the challenges for the future. Application systems need to be built in a way that allows for rapidly implementing changes in the future. Real-time integrated systems provide an organization with the tools to build products based on market demand, not what is most efficient for production. Legacy system integration is a key technology hurdle. Business applications within an entire value chain must be designed to exchange data seamlessly and operate in concert.

■ **Design the technical architecture:** Exposing the technical infra-structure to customers adds new complexities and challenges. Technical architectures must be designed for reliability, availability, performance, scalability, flexibility, manageability, and security. The technical infrastructure must be simplified, standardized, integrated, and automated. The penalty for systems failures is greater than ever, resulting in lost customers, decreasing stock prices, bad publicity, or even government action.

■ **Train the organization:** Training cannot be underestimated. The organization must be trained in new processes, new technology, new expectations, and new ways of doing business. E-business can impact the organization structures, culture, job responsibilities, and titles of individuals. Many times, new processes and technology fail because the organization fails to recognize and manage the human components of the change.

BENEFITS

Market and technology changes are rapidly changing the dynamics of competition. To be competitive, organizations must be both effective and efficient. Companies can establish a competitive advantage with e-business by optimizing the value chain and improving the effectiveness of the demand chain.

The value chain can be optimized by developing a powerful, efficient, and collaborative web of companies who individually and as a whole provide unique value to the customer. New products and services can be introduced to the market in a fraction of the time it takes now. Using e-business, processes throughout the organization and through the value chain can be streamlined to reduce costs and improve efficiency. The entire organization and value chain can be designed to react faster to competition. A powerful Intranet can provide improved communication to employees and drastically improve internal processes. A robust Extranet can improve the communication, interface, and processes with various partners in the value chain.

Competition for customer loyalty is greater than ever. The demand chain can be controlled and improved by the ability to identify, acquire, and retain profitable customers. Customer support and service can be designed to result in delighted customers. Critical to success in the new era is to understand customer needs and have a flexible and agile organization that can meet changing requirements. Use e-business and information technology to effectively manage and improve customer relationships.

In the new era, the power has shifted to the customer. Today, customers have information, power, and the ability to choose with whom they do business and how. Businesses no longer have a single distribution channel. Information from various distribution channels and customer points of contact must be synchronized and integrated. Organizations must meet customer expectations for speed and ease of doing business by providing customers with choices on how to interact with the organization. A company can now tell its message directly to the customer rather than hiding it behind other channels. The Internet provides a valuable additional channel to a company's already existing channel infrastructure. The Internet can improve communication and be used to provide and obtain information. In the past, it may have taken weeks or months to announce a new rebate program to customers or obtain valuable customer feedback. With the Internet, these can be done instantly!

Using the Internet, companies can immediately expand their marketplaces and become global. Using e-business, companies can increase their market shares and take business away from the competition. However, a business can also just as easily lose market share to competition, as competition is just a click away.

Companies must develop an e-business strategy to deliver greater total value to the customer by continuously improving the customer experience and relationship. A customer-led organization obtains its business strategy from its customers. The requirements for success increase as customer expectations increase. By revising value propositions to consistently provide customers with more value than the competition, revenues and profits will increase. Successful companies will make continuous learning and continuous benchmarking core competencies. Many resources offer additional information on the Internet. In addition to many useful books, there is a wealth of information available on the Internet. The following is a list of just a few of the many sites that provide up-to-date Internet information:

- www.internet.com
- www.allnetresearch.internet.com
- www.cyberatlas.com
- www.isoc.org
- www.w3.org
- www.cnet.com
- www.commerce.net

The time to act is now. In e-business, time means money and, in many cases, survival. What do customers want from your organization? The Internet is the portal through which the world views your company. What do you want the world to see and do? Use technology and e-business to create a positive customer experience as well as a competitive advantage over the competition. How will your organization respond to the significant business changes brought about by the Internet and e-business?

KEY POINTS TO REMEMBER

- Identify a clear e-business leader.
- Allocate necessary resources for success.
- Establish process so the organization plans and acts quickly.
- Redesign the business model.
- Design from the customer viewpoint.
- Redesign processes.
- Integrate the business applications.
- Design the technical architecture for reliability, availability, performance, scalability, flexibility, manageability, and security.
- Train the organization.
- Assess if the e-business efforts have achieved the desired benefits.

NOTES FOR MY E-BUSINESS EFFORT

APPENDICES

A. KEY QUESTIONS TO ASK FOR E-BUSINESS

CHAPTER 1: INTRODUCTION TO E-BUSINESS

- How have or will the business trends, application trends, and technical trends impact the organization, industry, and customers?
- Has the organization considered the e-business impact to the business model?
- Does the organization have a solid current business plan, e-business strategy, and information systems strategy in place?
- Why have the company's e-business ventures been successful or not?
- What company in the industry has been successful with e-business? Why has it been successful?

CHAPTER 2: E-BUSINESS PLANNING OVERVIEW

- Do you agree with the basic principles of the planning process presented in this book?
- Are there any additional sections that are necessary for the table of contents for the e-business plan?

CHAPTER 3: PHASE 1—BEGIN

Obtain Support:

- Is executive management ready to address the business planning and business model questions that will arise?
- Is management willing to invest the time and money to see the project through implementation?
- Is there a strong visionary business sponsor who is willing to be involved?
- Does management need to be educated and enlightened on the impact of e-business?
- Is executive management convinced of the impact that the Internet can have on the business?

Purpose:

- What has happened or what has changed to cause concern about the current state of affairs? Have several e-business projects and initiatives been completed, but lacked an overall strategy, direction, and framework needed to encompass the initiatives and establish the roadmap for the future?

- What is the problem? Why is a plan or strategy necessary?
- What are the demands? What must be done? How was the effort initiated? How was the need perceived?
- Why will the current methods not meet the demands?
- What is the consequence of staying status quo? What will happen if an e-business strategy and plan are not developed?
- How will the organization know if the effort is successful? What are the guiding goals to developing an e-business plan? Is the purpose of the document to communicate the company's vision, direction, and objectives relative to e-business? Is the result of the process to understand the current e-business situation and identify e-business opportunities?
- What is the scope of the effort and the plan? Does it include all divisions, all geographic areas, and all parts of the business?

Identify T0eam:

- Does the organization have the appropriate resources that can be allocated to planning and executing an e-business strategy?
- If not, what partner can best help the company succeed?

Planning Process:

- What process will be utilized to develop the e-business plan?
- What are the underlying principles of the planning process?
- What phases are included in the process?
- What sections should be included in the table of contents of the plan document?
- How will the plan be kept up to date on an ongoing basis?
- How is the e-business planning process integrated with the company's business planning process and information systems' planning process?
- Who is involved in the development of e-business plan?
- What are the individual responsibilities of each member involved in the development? Is accountability clearly identified?
- Who is responsible for the ongoing maintenance of the e-business plan and what are that individual's specific responsibilities?
- Who has decision-making authority on the e-business initiatives and direction?
- What is the process for obtaining funding for e-business initiatives?

Communication Plan:

- How will the organization be kept abreast of the vision, strategy, plans, and progress?

- How will team members be kept informed of progress and decisions?
- How frequently will team meetings be held? What will be their purpose and who will participate?
- How will the executive sponsor be kept up to date?
- How will decisions be made?

Announce:

- Why is e-business important to the organization?
- What process will be utilized to develop an e-business strategy?
- What is the time frame on when a strategy will be defined?
- What is the time frame on when initial projects will be implemented?
- Who will be involved in the effort? Why were they selected?
- How will others within the organization be impacted?

CHAPTER 4: PHASE 2—DIAGNOSE

Trends:

- Has the organization experienced a shift from a cost reduction strategy to a business growth strategy? Should this shift have occurred? Does the company have the proper balance of cost reduction and business growth to be successful?
- Is there an increased speed at which business must occur? Is the company operating quickly enough?
- Has the company shifted from being self-contained to a global organization? If not, what additional changes are required to become a global organization?
- Has the company experienced increased collaboration within the industry? Who are the partners with whom the organization is collaborating? What is the networked web of value?
- Has the company changed from economies of scale to one-to-one relationships? How has this impacted the internal business processes?
- Has the business focus shifted from internal to external? How?
- Do customers have the ability for self-service? Does it need to be improved?
- Is there an increased importance of processes? What are the critical processes?
- What impact does the shift to virtual offices have on the company?
- How have organizational structures changed to meet external requirements? How do they need to change to meet future requirements?

- Has technology become a critical enabler to business rather than an afterthought?
- What additional business trends impact the company?
- Are improvements necessary in the areas of
  - Enterprise Requirements Planing (ERP)?
  - Customer Relationship Management (CRM)?
  - Supply Chain Management (SCM)?
  - Enterprise Application Integration (EAI)?
  - Changing Technical Infrastructure?
  - Knowledge Management (KM)?
  - Return on Investment (ROI) Applications?
  - Communication Applications?
- What additional business application trends impact the company?
- What network improvements can be utilized in your company:
  - Increased connectivity?
  - Telecommunication advances?
  - Voice, data, video integration?
  - Increased use and reliance on Internet?
- What server improvements can be utilized at your company:
  - Decreased cost of a business transaction?
  - Increased interoperability and communication among diverse platforms?
  - Object-oriented programming?
  - Data synchronization ability?
  - Increased use of Java, HTML, XML, and other Web development and thin-client technologies?
  - Improved graphics, video, and sound?
  - Executive information systems?
  - Use of application service providers?
- What desktop and peripheral improvements can be utilized at your company:
  - Embedded, smaller, and more powerful processors and chips?
  - Wireless, cellular, and mobile technology?
  - Easy-to-use interfaces?
  - Voice recognition?
  - Multi-modal access, hand-held and PDA devices?
  - Computer telephone integration?
  - Pen-based computers and other mobile devices?
  - Bar coding?
  - Smart cards?
  - Encryption, biometrics, and other security measures?
- What additional technology trends impact the company?

Current Situation:

- What functionality does the Intranet/Internet/Extranet currently have? Outline the general areas of information and purpose. How much is the Intranet/Internet/Extranet used?
- What is the technical environment that supports the Intranet/Internet/Extranet? Identify the hardware server, operating system, and version.
- What people support the Intranet/Internet/Extranet environment? What do they do? What are their individual responsibilities?
- What processes support the Intranet/Internet/Extranet environment, directly or indirectly? How are changes made? How are changes prioritized? How are changes tested?

Situation Analysis:

- How does the company rate each of the areas on the e-business scorecard?

Stakeholders:

- Who are all the stakeholders, including customers, suppliers, public, employees, partners, and government?
- Who are the direct customers?
- Who are the indirect customers? Who are the end customers?
- What are the categories of customers and the amount of sales and transactions?
- Who are the potential customers?
- Who are the customers desired in the future?
- What are the most profitable customer segments today and in the future?
- How static is the customer base?
- What are the demographics of the current customer base?
- What is the purchase and interaction history of current customers?
- Which groups have the most influence on customer purchasing decisions?
- What customers generate referrals?
- What is the customer retention rate?
- What is the customer retention rate for targeted customers?
- What are customer service costs by customer segment?
- Does the organization have a single accurate database of all the customer information that is necessary? If not, how can it be developed?
- Who are the suppliers?
- What are the categories of suppliers and the amount of business transactions and cost?

- Who in the public would be interested in the company? Why?
- Who are the key partners? How beneficial or critical are these partners?
- Who are the key partners desired in the future?
- What government agencies have an impact on the company?
- What are the interests of customers?
- Why do customers come to the organization?
- Are customers happy with the business? Why or why not?
- Who else have customers considered for their needs? Why?
- How can the Internet help the business to give customers what they want?
- What do potential customers want?
- What are the preferences as to how customers want to be treated?
- What makes customers successful today? What will make them successful in the future?
- Is the business getting true customer input to really know what customers want?
- How can new customers be acquired?
- How can customers be retained?
- How can existing customer accounts be grown?
- What would customers change about the relationship with the company if they could?
- What new advances could benefit customers that they may not realize are possible?

Stakeholder's Processes:

- What steps or processes do customers (indirect or end customers) go through to select and buy the product or service?
- What steps or processes do the direct customers go through to select and buy the product or service?
- How does the company interact with customers?
- How can the customer process be streamlined?
- What steps or processes do suppliers go through to have a relationship with the company?
- How can the suppliers' processes be streamlined?
- Does the business have control over the customer's entire process?
- What topics of information is the public interested in?
- What topics of information do employees need?
- How often do the stakeholders (including customers, suppliers, others) use the Internet? How technology literate or averse are the stakeholders?
- What are the various points of interaction that the company may have with the customer and various stakeholders?
- How can the company engage customers in the order, production, and delivery process?

Industry Analysis:

- Who are the competitors?
- What are each competitor's strengths and weaknesses?
- Are there a lot of competitors or a few large competitors? What companies dominate the industry? How might this change in the future?
- What might competition look like in the future due to market expansion, product expansion, backward integration, forward integration, change in fortune, or e-business?
- What is the total industry size today? In the future?
- What are the distribution channels?
- What changes or technologies would revolutionize the industry if they were implemented?
- What future technologies will impact the industry?
- What are the greatest e-business threats to the business?
- How can the Internet change the business?
- What impact will e-business have on the retail channel and the distribution channel?
- What impact will e-business have on the price structure?
- What impact will e-business have on existing business?
- What channel expansion or disintermediation is possible?
- What types of distribution channel conflict may arise?
- What is the company's channel strategy?
- What companies are allies?
- How can the company reach new customers and new markets?
- What is the impact on marketing and branding strategies?
- Are there any governmental or regulatory changes impacting the industry?
- What are barriers to entry in the market? For example, high capital costs, high customer switching costs, strong customer loyalty, regulation, and patents.
- What are barriers to exit in the market? For example, expensive equipment that is difficult to sell, long-term labor contracts, extended customer leases, service agreements, and government regulations.
- What other alternatives do customers have for the product?
- Do market assumptions need to be redefined?

Value Chain:

- What are the steps in the value chain?
- Where are the weak links in the value chain?
- What is the role of the business in the value chain?
- Can the company work with others to add more value more efficiently?

- Do others have assets the company can utilize?
- What impact will increased connectivity have on the value of your brand?
- How can the entire value stream be re-engineered?
- How can steps be simplified? Can steps be combined?
- Can the order of steps be changed?
- Can the process be accelerated? Can the timing change?
- Have parallel industries cut major steps from the process? How?

Business Analysis:

- What are the internal strengths of the business? Are there any new strengths relative to e-business and Internet capabilities?
- What is the business good at doing?
- What capabilities, resources, and skills can the business draw upon to carry out the strategies?
- Why do customers buy from the company?
- What is the company's competitive advantage?
- Why do employees stay at the company?
- Consider and rate the critical areas, such as management, organization, customer base, research and development, operations, sales and marketing, distribution and delivery, and financial condition.
- What are the internal weaknesses of the business?
- What is the business not good at doing?
- What deficiencies may hinder the business from achieving the strategies?
- Why might the company lose a sale or customer?
- Why do employees quit the company?
- What are possible shifts in technology with e-business and Internet?
- How might availability of new materials change with e-business?
- What are new customer categories with the Internet-enabled world?
- Why might there be sudden spurts or changes in market growth?
- Are there any new uses for old product?
- Can the business get access to highly skilled people through the use of Internet technology?
- Can the business reach new locations and geographies with the Internet?
- Would any new organization models be useful?
- Are there any new distribution channels available as a result of the Internet?
- Are there any potential changes to laws or regulations?
- Might there be market slowdowns?
- Is there any legislation that might be costly?
- Are there any changing trends due to technology?

- Is new and aggressive competition resulting from the Internet?
- Are there substitute products?
- Is there exchange-rate volatility?
- Might there be a shortage of any raw material?
- Are there any potential changes in patent protections?
- Are there any potential changes in labor agreements?
- Has the product saturated the market?

CHAPTER 5: PHASE 3—DEVELOP

Value Proposition:

- What does the customer value? Does the customer value cross-selling, up-selling, new or updated products and services, supply chain efficiencies, decreased cycle times, or faster time-to-market? Go back to the list of items in Chapter 4 that were identified as potential desires of a customer. Which of these are important to customers?
- What does the customer not value and is unwilling to pay for?
- What does the customer not value today but will in the future?
- What value would delight customers and exceed their expectations?
- How will e-business change the customer expectations?
- How can a new value proposition be created for the customer?
- What new forms of value can be created?
- How can the business build loyalty and maintain customers in the connected economy? How can the customer be encouraged to do business with the business and not with competitors?
- What do customers have in common? How could they gain value from one another in a community?

Value Delivery Proposition:

- How is the business positioned to deliver the value?
- How is the competition positioned to deliver the value?
- Can other entities provide the same value?
- How can the business model change to better deliver the value?
- Can the business expand value by moving up or down the distribution channel?
- Can the business transform from a commodity offering to a total experience offering?
- Can the business change the delivery of the value?
- What challenges or barriers will the company face?

- How can the business be designed to meet customer expectations?
- How can the customer experience be improved?
- Can the business create a totally new experience for the customer?
- How can the business make the product/service faster?
- How can the business make the product/service more convenient?
- How can the business make the product/service more personalized or custom? How can the business deliver personalized service?
- How can the business offer the product/service at a lower price?
- How can the business offer the product/service at higher quality?
- How can the business own the customer's total experience? How much control does the business have over the total customer experience (including learning about productions, selecting, quoting, purchasing, delivery, setup, installation, after-care, service, purchasing follow-on products, taking delivery, invoicing, resolving disputes.)
- Does the business provide a 360-degree view of the customer relationship (i.e., whoever takes the call has access to records of the customer relationship even if it is with another department)? Can the customer access information about all his or her accounts or issues?
- Can customers help themselves?
- How can the business utilize technology to do things it is not currently doing?
- How can the business increase flexibility and responsiveness?
- How can the business be more efficient and effective?
- How can the customer process be streamlined?
- How can the business take advantage of the strengths and minimize the weaknesses? How can the business aggressively take advantage of the opportunities and diminish the threats?
- How can the business impact the competitors and industry?
- How can the business re-engineer the value chain?

Strategy:

- How will the business create value in the future? Is it to reach more and new types of customers, providing cross-selling and up-selling? Is it through new or updated products or services, new packaging and pricing approaches? Is it through supply, service, or distribution chain efficiencies? Is it through decreased cycle times, faster time-to-market?
- How can the business use e-business to meet customer needs as well as the business goals and objectives?
- Is the business a market leader or follower? Where does the business want to be?

- Will the business take an aggressive e-business approach to e-enabling the entire enterprise and processes, or will it utilize e-business in a targeted approach to provide information, enhance service, facilitate transactions, or provide community?
- What are the driving objectives the business will utilize e-business to accomplish? For example, is the business going to use e-business to reduce costs, generate leads, increase revenue, improve communication, develop brand, enable new business models, launch a new product, or train employees?
- What new opportunities does the Internet provide?
- What additional markets can the company reach?
- What does the business do well to satisfy customers and how can it be ported and exploited in the electronic playing field of the Internet?
- What role can the Internet play in helping the company meet the value proposition and value delivery proposition? What role can the Intranet play? What role can the Extranet play?
- Is the business strategy to meet customer values by achieving operational excellence, customer intimacy, or technical superiority?
- With what partners and suppliers will the business need to align?
- How can the business build trust and share among partners?
- What is the true core identity of the business? Disassemble or outsource those activities not core, assemble those that are core. What can be separated or outsourced?
- What is the business doing that it shouldn't be doing?
- Has e-business changed what the company does, what groups of customers are served, what products or services are provided, or what sets the business apart from competition?
- Has e-business changed where the company is going or what it is going to become?
- Has e-business and designing the strategy from the outside in changed how the company wants to articulate the values?
- Do the goals need to change in light of thinking from the outside in?
- Do the objectives change as a result of e-business? Are the stated levels of ambition, goals, and objectives high enough or do they need to be reset? Can the objectives be accomplished more quickly with e-business initiatives?

Metrics:

- Review the value proposition. What do the customers and business value?
- How can that value be measured?
- What are the desired effects of e-business on the organization?

CHAPTER 6: PHASE 4—DEFINE

Opportunities:

- For each stakeholder and each step of his/her process, what can the company do specifically to meet the value statements identified?
- What information needs are necessary?

Competitive Situation:

- What was learned from a detailed review of competitor's Web sites?
- Which company had the best site? Which had the worst site? Does this make sense when you consider what is known about the companies?
- Overall, how did your company's site compare to the competitors' sites?
- Which competitors had the greatest breadth or addressed the most opportunities?
- Which competitors had the greatest depth and content?
- How many opportunities had no competitor addressed? Review these for potential competitive advantages.
- Which stakeholders had the most complete scores? For example, were the majority of ratings for the public higher than the ratings for the end customer? It may be an opportunity to more thoroughly address the needs for a particular stakeholder.
- Which process steps had the weakest scores? For example, was more functionality provided in recognizing the need than in service and support? It may be an opportunity to more thoroughly address the needs for a particular step in the process.
- What is the unique functionality that is covered today? What opportunities were addressed by just one company?
- What are the opportunities that no company covers today?
- How did navigation and screen design compare for each company?
- What companies had worldwide and language capabilities?
- Did it appear that any of the companies had Extranet functionality or areas that were restricted to members only by the use of an ID and password?
- What percent of the opportunities did no company address? How much opportunity is there to create a unique competitive differentiation in the market?
- What new opportunities were identified? How can one-to-one marketing be developed? How can customer loyalty be increased?
- Do you want to copy a successful competitor or re-invent the industry?

Priorities:

- Which prioritization method should the company utilize?
- At which stage is each of the identified opportunities?
- How can the company balance the risk, investment, difficulty, and competitive advantage by stages?
- Which opportunity was the most innovative and unique to the industry?
- Which opportunities are the easiest to implement?
- What opportunities will have the greatest impact on the business value and objectives?
- Which opportunities would be the best for the organization to pursue?
- How would the customers rank the priorities?

CHAPTER 7: PHASE 5—DETERMINE

Business Application:

- What information architecture is needed to support the requirements?
- What application architecture is needed to support the e-business model and customer requirements?
- What applications require integration to be successful?
- What application modules must be e-enabled, and what is the relative priority?
- Which applications contribute significantly to the business and which ones require disproportionate support?
- What applications can be connected directly to customers in order to improve the flow?
- How can e-mail interactions with customers be automated?
- How can e-mail, phone, and Internet interactions be integrated?
- How can the various customer touch-points be integrated?
- What information should be available to better support the business decisions?
- What applications can be connected directly to suppliers in order to improve the flow?
- How can a closer interface be obtained with suppliers and the value chain to forecast demand and schedule more accurately?
- How can costs be decreased?
- Does the organization have a common language, definitions, rules, goals, and commitment? What are the business hurdles?
- Does the organization have any issues doing business without any boundaries (e.g., sales territories, plants, countries, languages, or cultures)?

- For e-business to succeed, what impact or coordination will be required with the parent company, sister companies, divisions, distribution channel, suppliers, and partners?

Technical Architecture:

- What technical infrastructure must be in place to support the e-business requirements?
- What are the speed, stability, and availability requirements?
- What are the service-level requirements?
- What are the bandwidth requirements?
- What are the computing resource requirements?
- Is there sufficient hardware (firewalls, network switches, servers, network lines) in place for the potential traffic? Has bandwidth and server capacity been estimated at many times the average load?
- Are there any single points of failure in the architecture?
- Has replication been considered? How often will replication take place and what is the cost?
- Has mirroring been considered to keep copies dynamically up to date?
- Is the architecture scalable?
- Have redundancy, load balancing, and clustering been considered? Can the capacity in a cluster handle the additional load if a component goes down?
- Have caching and distribution of data and graphics been considered?
- Has a network policy been developed with priorities identified?
- Are there both real-time and historical performance measurement and monitoring tools available? Are they used consistently? Who reviews the data? How frequently? What action is taken?
- Is security sufficient?
- Who gets access? When do they get access? How do they get access?
- Is security administration distributed or centralized?
- How is self-administration minimized while still keeping the environment secure?
- How is management alerted to security breaches or issues?
- How is loss or corruption of data prevented during transmission?
- Have software and hardware components been selected from reputable, solid, and secure vendors?
- What support levels are provided by each vendor?

Business Processes:

- What business processes need to change to handle the e-business customer expectations?

- How can business processes be integrated throughout the value chain?
- Are the business processes automated?
- Are the business processes and information fully integrated?
- Do the processes cross throughout the organization?
- Does each process have metrics to measure the effectiveness and efficiency of the process?
- How does the organization know if processes are broken or need improvement?
- Is there a culture of continuous improvement?
- Are processes designed to do the right work and to do the work right the first time? Are processes designed to prevent errors?
- How can best practices of the various business units be combined?
- Do processes have corrective action designed so that the root cause is determined and fixed?
- Are processes documented and followed consistently?
- How can the processes be streamlined from the outside in, from the customer's perspective? Look at product configuration, manufacturing, shipment and delivery, presales and postsales service, billing, and credit-checking.
- Are orders processed quickly enough?
- Can items be ordered from multiple divisions?
- How can the direct customer interfacing processes be streamlined?
- How do the product and order process look from a customer standpoint?
- Is customer satisfaction measured and acted upon on a regular basis?
- Is the customer profile companywide? Who ensures its accuracy?
- How will leads be pursued and turned into sales?
- How quickly will questions and requests be handled?
- How will information provided on registrations be utilized?
- How will Internet sales be compensated?
- What process will be utilized to update content on the Web site?
- How will employees be kept aware of changing content?
- Is the process defined, documented, and understood by all process participants?
- Does the process have an owner who is responsible for its performance?
- Can the process be measured?
- Are metrics from the process reviewed on a regular basis and appropriate action taken?
- Is user satisfaction measured for the process on a regular basis by asking those who receive output from the process?
- Is the process automated with tools?
- Is the process optimized to reduce unnecessary interventions and wait times?

- Is each activity in the process necessary?
- Is the process improved on a regular basis?
- Are roles and responsibilities documented?
- Does the process cross the organization or the supply chain? Has it been optimized?

Information Systems Processes

- How do the information systems processes need to change to support the e-business requirements?
- Are capacity and storage managed properly to meet the volatile e-business needs?
- What are the service-level requirements? Is the organization meeting them?
- Is change control complete enough? Have changes been implemented with no impact?
- Are systems and data backed up on a regular basis? Does a disaster recovery plan exist? Has it been tested?
- What is the mean time to fix issues? Is the problem management quick enough to handle e-business issues with minimal impact?
- Are hardware and software documented and upgrades planned without issue?
- Are jobs documented and run successfully and uneventfully?
- Is software distribution managed and executed properly?
- Are systems developed and projects completed on time, on budget, and meeting the required functionality?
- Is the Information Systems organization integrated seamlessly with the business? Are internal customers satisfied with the support and communication from Information Systems?
- Are facilities managed to minimize risk and issues?
- Are finances controlled and managed to provide a positive return?
- Are vendors managed properly to minimize cost and optimize the value chain?
- Does Information Systems have a direction that is aligned with the business direction?
- Is security managed to minimize risk and disruption to the business?
- Are assets managed to obtain the lowest total cost of ownership?
- Are key business and technical statistics being gathered, reported, and managed?
- Are owners of services well defined?
- Are processes regularly improved?
- Are employees satisfied?

People/Organization:

- What is the required skill set for developing and implementing the e-business systems?
- What is the required skill set to support the e-business systems?
- Does the organization have the necessary skill set and resources that can be allocated to developing and implementing the e-business systems?
- Who in the business is responsible for content development and updating? Is it recognized as part of that individual's job?
- How will e-business impact the sales force?
- Who will respond to questions that are submitted on the Web site?
- Who will respond to literature requests?
- Who will compile information provided on registrations?
- Who will update customer lists?
- Who will monitor and improve customer satisfaction?
- What orientation and training is required?
- Are there sufficient resources assigned?
- Are new or changed responsibilities defined and documented?
- Is there appropriate backup of responsibilities and knowledge for the business areas?
- How will the performance of individuals be measured? How about the performance of the group?
- What incentives are needed to encourage and promote e-solutions in the organization? Do incentives match the goals?
- Are cross-functional teams in place to improve e-business processes?

Cost/Benefit:

- How much will hardware cost for the infrastructure improvements that are necessary?
- Is there any service provider cost?
- How much will software cost for the necessary infrastructure improvements?
- How much will the internal and external labor cost to make the necessary infrastructure improvements?
- How much will the software cost for the business application improvements that are necessary?
- How much will the internal and external labor cost for the business application improvements?
- How much will training cost to support the business applications as well as process changes that are necessary? How much travel cost is required for the training?

- How much will it cost for re-engineering the business processes?
- How much will the interfaces to other applications or organizations cost?
- How much will the conversions cost?
- What are the opportunity costs? What will not get completed as a result of focusing resources on e-business?
- What are the total costs?
- What are the one-time costs?
- What are the recurring costs?
- How much should the organization expect to allocate to keeping e-business abreast of market and customer changes on an ongoing basis?
- What are the unquantifiable or qualitative costs that will be incurred?
- What will be the cost if the organization does not implement the e-business strategy? Will the company fall behind the competition?
- Why is the e-business effort required to support the business strategy?
- What is the estimated impact of improved customer satisfaction?
- How much will sales increase?
- How much will total costs decrease?
- What is the estimated benefit of increased process efficiencies?
- What is the estimated benefit of reduced transaction costs?
- What is the impact of reduced inventory?
- What is the impact of improved market presence, extending market reach?
- What is the impact of improved supplier interface?
- What is the impact on a reduced manufacturing cycle time?
- What is the impact of increased speed of transaction from order to ship?
- What is the impact to decreasing customer support costs?
- What is the impact on overhead costs?
- What are the total estimated benefits?
- What are the unquantifiable or qualitative benefits that will be realized?
- Are there risks associated with the development time?
- Are there risks associated with the resources?
- Are there risks associated with the resources required in ongoing support of the organization?
- Are there risks associated with the scope of the project?
- Are there risks associated with tasks that cannot be easily measured?
- What is the greatest risk, delay in implementation or accuracy and completeness of a Web site?

Roadmap:

- How much money can the organization afford to spend per year on e-business?
- How quickly must the organization achieve the strategic vision?
- How well can the organization implement and adapt to change?
- What opportunities will achieve the greatest benefit?
- Are projects scheduled for completion in 3 to 5 months or less?
- Does each project have a defined deliverable, with a beginning and an end?
- Will the initial projects provide a positive momentum for the e-business effort?
- Will the initial projects provide a payback greater than the cost of the project within a year?

Approval:

- Why is e-business critical for the company?
- What is happening in the industry to warrant concern?
- What is the current status of e-business for the company?
- How does the current state of e-business compare with the competition?
- Are there major changes planned to the value chain?
- What are major changes to the business plan?
- Who are the customers?
- What is the value proposition?
- What is a summary of the e-business strategy?
- What is the total number of e-business opportunities that were identified?
- What is the total cost of the e-business projects? What is the cost over the next year? 2 years?
- What is the total benefit of the e-business projects?
- What is the return on investment?
- What can the company expect to accomplish with e-business?

CHAPTER 8: PHASE 6—DESIGN

Look and Feel:

- Is there something on the main page to get the customer's attention and engage interest? How can the organization capture and seduce the intended audience?
- How can the organization establish a positive relationship? How can it be a comfortable experience for the customer?

- How can the organization get customers to return? How can it be memorable?
- How can the organization create a meaningful personal relationship?
- Does the site invite customers, welcome them, and help them to be effective?
- Does the design enhance and communicate the corporate image and establish the organization's brand?

Navigation:

- Are the search and contact us functions in an easy-to-find spot on every screen?
- Is navigation that takes the customer away from the site avoided?
- Is there always a clear path back to the home page?
- Are buttons clearly and concisely labeled?
- Is navigation consistent?
- Do the visitors always have a sense of where they are within the site?
- Does navigation take a minimal amount of space?
- Is navigation simple?

Screens:

- How will the organization reinforce its image?
- How can emphasis be added?
- Is the message as easy to read as possible (e.g., effective use of columns, typeface, type size, alignment, line spacing, white space, punctuation, capitalization, text wraps, word spacing, color)?
- Does the content have the information in which customers would be interested?
- Is the mix of text and graphics or visuals pleasing?
- Does the screen catch the customer's attention or get involvement?
- Does the screen provide the image that is desired to communicate (e.g., conservative, contemporary, cheap, expensive, quiet, dignified, flamboyant, formal, informal)?
- Is the site fresh with some time-sensitive information? Does the site give the users something to come back for?

Applications:

- Can accurate information be provided to the customer online and quickly?
- How can marketing efforts be automated to improve efficiency?

- How can the sales force processes be automated to improve efficiency?
- How can call centers and customer databases be integrated?
- How can customer responses and profiles be automated, and quotes and proposals be managed throughout the process?
- How can the order management process be automated so the organization is easy to do business with?
- How can a transparent interface be provided to the customer throughout the process from product design to product delivery?
- How can the information flow be improved and overall product costs be reduced by improving the flow of goods through production?
- How can lead times be reduced, quality increased, and customization enabled at a lower cost?
- How can inventory be replaced with improved information?

Security:

- How likely is a security breach?
- What are the consequences of a security issue or breach?
- How much processing and cost are justified to counter security threats?
- What groups of individuals cannot see other groups of individuals' information? This includes other geographies, other stakeholders, and other partners.
- What information should be secured?
- Are the programmers following secure programming practices?
- Are security policies enforced at the application level before input gets to the e-business software?

CHAPTER 9: PHASE 7—DELIVER

Develop:

- Is the project team a solid high-performing and a well-functioning team?
- Are roles and responsibilities of team members clearly identified?
- Are resources committed to the project at the level anticipated throughout the life of the project?
- Are the business requirements and customer needs understood by everyone?
- Has quality been sacrificed?
- Is the scope realistic and managed?
- Are trade-offs of time, cost, and quality managed and communicated?

- Are risks managed?
- Is a project methodology consistently utilized?
- Does each project have a documented project plan with a schedule, identified team, and documented responsibilities?
- Are there small deliverable tasks?
- Does each task have one person responsible with a planned deliver date?
- Are deadlines aggressive, but not unrealistic?
- Does the project plan consider training and process changes that will be necessary?
- Does the project plan consider integration issues to back office and front office systems?
- Is communication frequent, open, and honest throughout the project team, business, and management?
- Is the status of each task frequently reviewed?
- Are weekly project management meetings held to review the previous week's deliverables and discuss the deliverables for the next week?
- Are team meetings documented? Are issues documented and acted upon?
- Does the team utilize proven technology or do a proof of concept?
- Whenever possible, are vendor-supplied packages utilized rather than writing custom software?
- Is software modeled or prototyped whenever possible?
- Is application development done in an iterative, incremental approach with frequent release cycles?
- Whenever possible, does the team use objects or re-usable code that has been tested?
- Does the team use a source code peer-review process?
- Are post-project reviews completed to analyze if the business benefits were achieved?

Test:

- Were all the business processes tested?
- Were connectivity issues tested?
- Were all the locations tested?
- Were any fixes tested?
- Was testing performed on different clients and different hardware?
- Were different browsers and browser releases (Internet Explorer, Netscape Navigator, etc.) tested?
- Were different resolutions (640 × 480, 800 × 600, 1024 × 768) tested?
- Were different color depths (256, 16-bit, 24-bit) tested?
- Were different operating systems (Windows releases, Mac releases) tested?

- Were different connection speeds (14.4 KB, 56 KB) tested?
- Was security tested?
- Was a stress test completed?
- Was the contingency plan tested?

Train:

- Have all the individuals involved in the new business processes been identified?
- Do all the individuals understand their new roles, expectations, and metrics upon which they will be measured?
- Do all the individuals understand the business direction and priorities, and what they mean to them and their jobs?
- Have all the individuals been trained in the new business process?
- Have all the individuals been trained in the new technology?
- Have the Information Systems individuals been trained properly in the new technology?
- Have the Information Systems individuals been trained properly in the new processes?
- Have any organization changes been communicated to the individuals impacted as well as the organization?
- Have procedures and documentation been updated for employees to reference?
- Do you have the acceptance, involvement, and commitment of the organization to make e-business successful?

Implement:

- Who will respond to questions that are submitted? What is the process? How quickly will questions be responded to?
- Who will respond to requests for literature and additional information? What is the process? How quickly will requests be responded to? Who will follow-up leads for potential sales?
- Who will compile the information received on registration forms and update customer files? What will the information be used for? Is all the information present that is required?
- What are the disaster recovery plan and business continuity plan? Have they been tested?
- Does the culture support the business objectives of customer satisfaction?
- Has the organization invested in proactive capacity planning and change simulation tools?
- Has the organization invested in real-time availability and performance management tools?

- As volume cannot be predicted, is excess capacity maintained? Is load balancing in place with the ability to add more capacity as needed?
- Has the architecture been planned to enable scheduled downtime for portions of the system while minimizing overall impact?
- Is there no single point of failure, including the technical architecture, applications, people, or processes? Has redundancy been designed?

Promote:

- Does the site show up near the top of major search engines?
- Is the URL included everywhere, including marketing literature, presentations, business cards, brochures, e-mail signatures, invoices, communications, annual report, letters, news releases, radio ads, television ads, directories, voice mail, side of van, and side of building?
- Has the Web site been added to the voice mail system as an option for customers?
- Have alliances been leveraged by cross promotions and links?
- Have you considered purchasing links from industry sites?
- Have you found complementary Web sites and tried to establish reciprocal links?
- Have you considered beginning an affiliate program that has a financial stake in promoting your site?
- Have you considered joining an e-mall site?
- Is the site promoted in mailing lists and news groups?
- Have you considered a banner exchange program or purchasing banner advertising?
- Have you considered purchasing advertising in e-mail newsletters?
- Have you considered renting targeted e-mail lists?
- Have you prepared a handout, mailing insert, and e-mail announcement to promote the Web site?
- Have you made a media announcement?
- Has promotion been considered in the design of the site? Do visitors have a reason to come back?
- Does someone within the organization have the responsibility for ongoing promotion and marketing?

CHAPTER 10: PHASE 8—DISCUSS

Obtain Feedback:

- Does the initial screen catch the customer's interest?
- What do customers think of the Internet screens and functionality?
- Do the Internet pages download quickly?

- Are there reasons for visitors to register at the site?
- Is quality of content good?
- Is content up to date and fresh?
- Can visitors find the information they need?
- Is the site organized how the customer would use it?
- Can visitors search for information?
- Is it easy for visitors to contact the company?
- Which pages are used the most and least? Is this what was expected?

Analyze

- Did the organization achieve the objectives that were stated in the Executive Summary, Introduction, Strategy, and Benefits sections?
- How does the organization rate now on the e-business scorecard originally developed in the Situation Analysis section?
- Is the organization achieving the metrics and targets that were identified in the Strategy section?
- What benefits were realized that were not identified in the plan?
- What expected benefits were not realized? Why not?
- Were the projects completed on time, within budget, delivering the planned functionality?
- What problems were encountered?
- What should be changed next time?
- What do customers want or ask for that is not currently provided?
- What, if anything, has changed in the market?
- How have competitors reacted?
- Does the e-business strategy require changes?
- What new functionality do competitors offer?
- Are performance, availability, and security sufficient?
- Are business processes functioning properly?
- Is site content updated?
- What new technology developments could be useful?
- Now that the organization has a better understanding of e-business, are there additional revenue opportunities or cost savings that weren't originally identified?

Determine Action:

- Has the appropriate level of resources, including budget and people, been assigned to update site content?
- Has the appropriate level of resources, including budget and people, been assigned to maintain and administer the e-business technical infrastructure?
- Are vendor releases kept current?

- Are changes in customer requirements considered and acted upon?
- Are changes in technology reviewed and acted upon?
- Is the planning process redone on a regular basis?

CHAPTER 11: SUMMARY

- Has a clear e-business leader been identified?
- Have proper resources been allocated?
- Does the organization plan and act quickly?
- Has the business model been redesigned?
- Has the organization been designed from the customer viewpoint?
- Have the processes been redesigned?
- Have the business applications been integrated?
- Has the technical architecture been designed for reliability, availability, performance, scalability, flexibility, manageability, and security?
- Has the organization been trained?
- Have the e-business efforts achieved the desired benefits? Why or why not?

B. SAMPLE TABLE OF CONTENTS FOR AN E-BUSINESS PLAN

I.   Executive Summary

{ One to two pages summarizing each section of the plan.

II.   Introduction
      A. Purpose of Document
      B. Planning Process

Outlines the purpose of the plan document, the process utilized for the initial development as well as the ongoing maintenance. It also identifies the individuals involved in e-business and outlines their specific responsibilities.

III. Trends

Outlines the trends in the industry that impact the organization. This includes business trends, business application, and technical trends.

IV.   Current Situation
      A. Intranet
      B. Internet
      C. Extranet

Outlines the current status of the Intranet, Internet, and Extranet environments for the company. For each environment, include the business functionality currently provided, the technical environment, the people supporting it with their responsibilities, and the processes supporting the environment. This section includes the facts of the current environments, without editorials or analysis of the issues.

V.   Situation Analysis
    A. Intranet
    B. Internet
    C. Extranet
    D. Scorecard
    E. Stakeholders
    F. Stakeholder Process
    G. Industry Analysis
    H. Value Chain
    I. Business Analysis

This section has the analysis or opinions of the current situation that was outlined above. It identifies the strengths and areas of improvement in the Intranet, Internet, and Extranet environments. Utilize a quantitative scorecard to communicate the status in various areas. All the stakeholders are identified as well as current and desired customers. Identify why they are customers, and what value the customers want the business to provide. Identify the decision process utilized by each stakeholder through the life of the relationship, beginning with deciding to do business with the company. Review and analyze the industry. Analyze and re-engineer the value chain. Analyze the business, including strengths, weaknesses, opportunities, and threats.

VI. Direction/Strategy
   A. Value Proposition
   B. Value Delivery
      Proposition
   C. Strategy
   D. Metrics

Define the value proposition or what value the company wants to provide to the stakeholders. A stakeholder is anyone who has an interest in the success or operation of the company, such as customers, shareholders, vendors, distributors, or the government. Define the tools or vehicle to deliver the value, the strategy and impact to the business plan, the desired business impact, as well as how to measure success.

VII. Opportunities
   A. Customers
   B. Partners and Suppliers
   C. Public
   D. People/Employees

Take each stakeholder and step in the decision-making process, ask how the company can achieve the value proposition in that step of the process. Answering this question will help identify various opportunities.

VIII. Competitive Situation

For each opportunity that was identified, review top competitors and rate how well they provide each particular functionality or opportunity. Then summarize the competitive situation and identify market opportunities and opportunities that will provide a competitive advantage.

IX. E-Business Requirements.
   A. Business Application
   B. Technical
      Infrastructure
   C. Information Systems
      Processes
   D. Business Processes
   E. People/Organization

Identify the specific action items and projects required to implement the e-business strategy and opportunities. There will be action items necessary in the areas of business applications, technical infrastructure, people/organization, information systems processes, and business processes.

X. Business Case
   A. Costs
   B. Benefits
   C. ROI

Although it may be nice if companies would hand over large sums of money for information systems projects without asking for the benefits or return on investment, this is typically not the case (as it should be). Any major effort typically requires identifying all the costs, benefits, and the return on investment.

XI. Roadmap

XII. Appendix

Prioritize and map the individual projects required to get to the end point. Each project should be less than three months, have a beginning and an end, with a specific deliverable and person responsible. Now that management knows where the company wants to be, they need to communicate to the employees the steps to get there.

AFTERWORD

For additional information, contact Strategic Computing Directions at:

acassidy@strategiccomputing.com
or
www.strategiccomputing.com
or
www.apracticalguide.com

Strategic Computing Directions, Incorporated is an executive information systems consulting organization dedicated to providing practical and proven solutions to information systems challenges. The focus of the organization includes:

- Strategic planning and e-business strategy development to identify how to use technology for a competitive advantage
- Current assessment to identify the areas of risk and improvement in an information systems organization
- Process re-engineering to improve the efficiency and effectiveness of an organization
- Major software and hardware selection and implementation to assist in implementing the strategic direction
- Temporary information systems leadership

We look forward to the opportunity to assist you on your e-business journey.

Other complementary books by Anita Cassidy include:

- *A Practical Guide to Information Systems Strategic Planning* (1998)
- *A Practical Guide to Information Systems Process Improvement* (2000) (with Keith Guggenberger)

INDEX

V

W

For Product Safety Concerns and Information please contact our EU
representative GPSR@taylorandfrancis.com Taylor & Francis Verlag GmbH,
Kaufingerstraße 24, 80331 München, Germany

Printed and bound by CPI Group (UK) Ltd, Croydon, CR0 4YY
08/05/2025
01864360-0005